GCSE Physics

Volume 3

Electricity, Electromagnetism and Nuclear Physics

Dr Asad Altimeemy

Preface

This book is the third and final volume of "GCSE Physics Grades 7-9". Like previous volumes, this book is designed to help the highest performing students achieve Grade 7 or above. It is the result of teaching Physics for last 23 years in secondary and tertiary education. I have always supported my students with extensive typed notes and fully worked answers and scaffolded exemplars. This book is a comprehensive study aid which includes notes and fully answered questions. It will help you check and consolidate your learning. The book covers the requirements for most exam boards. A thorough understanding of all the topics is required to master the skills to achieve Grades 8 or 9. To achieve these higher grades, you should make thorough notes and answer all the targeted questions independently. The book has 64 fully answered examples and questions to enable you to master these grades. Questions which have the * symbol are Grade 9 questions.

Dr Asad Altimeemy
B.Sc., Ph.D., P.G.C.E, M.Inst.P.

CONTENT

Chapter 1

Static Electricity

When you take off a jumper over a shirt made from manmade materials, we hear a crackling sound. A plastic ruler rubbed with a piece of cloth will pick up small pieces of paper. You sometimes get a small electric shock when getting out of a car. In a thunder storm, there are huge flashes of lightning. All these things are due to static electricity.

Materials which are insulators can be charged by friction charging.

There are two types of electric charge:
- Positive
- Negative

Most objects are electrically neutral. This means that they have an equal number of positive and negative charges. To charge an object, one has to alter the charge balance of positive and negative charges. There are three ways to do it: friction, conduction and induction. Remember, in solid objects only negative charges, electrons, move.

Charging by Friction

Insulators can transfer charge by friction. When the surface of one insulator rubs against another, negative charge particles, electrons, can be transferred.

The insulator which gains electrons will get a negative charge; the insulator which loses electrons will get a positive charge. It is most important to know that it is only the electrons which can move. Positive charges cannot move because they are stuck inside the nuclei of the atoms of the material.

For example, if polythene (a type of plastic) is rubbed with a dry cloth, electrons are transferred from the cloth to the polythene. The polythene gains electrons and becomes negatively charged, the cloth loses electrons and becomes positively charged.

It is not possible to predict in advance which way the electrons will go for a certain material. The same cloth, when rubbed against acetate (a different type of plastic) will gain electrons and become negatively charged, leaving the acetate with a positive charge.

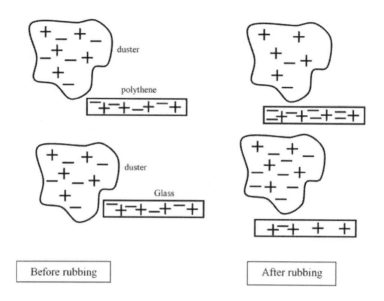

Before rubbing	After rubbing

The closer the charges get to each other, the bigger the attraction or repulsion becomes. This rule holds right down to the forces between particles inside atoms.

Charging by conduction

The charging by conduction process involves touching of a charged particle to a conductive material. This way the charges are transferred from the charged material to the conductor. This method is useful for charging conductors.

Charging by induction

A charged object is brought close to but does not touch the conductor. In the end, the conductor has charge of the opposite sign as the charge on the object.

2

To charge an object by induction:

- Bring the charged object close to, but not touching, the conductor. The charge on the conductor shifts in response to the nearby charged object.
- Connect the conductor to ground.
  Ground is basically a charge reservoir - anything that can give up or receive charge without noticing the change. Electrons flow from ground to the conductor if the charged object is positive, and the opposite way if the object is negative. The conductor now has a net charge with a sign opposite to the sign on the charged object.
- Remove the ground connection. The transferred electrons can't get back to where they came from.
- Remove the charged object. The net charge distributes itself over the surface of the conductor.

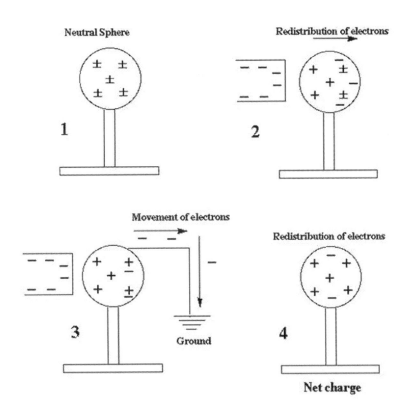

Attraction and Repulsion

Opposite charges attract. Like charges repel. This means that two positively or two negative charges charged things will repel each other; two negatively charged things will repel each other.

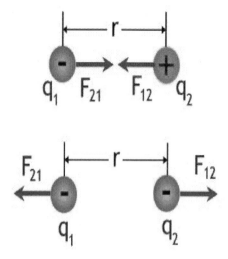

The further apart the charged are, the weaker the forces of attraction and repulsion are. To detect if the object is charged, use an electroscope.

Gold Leaf Electroscope

The electroscope is a very, very thin piece of gold foil fixed at the top to a piece of copper.

The copper has a large round top, called the cap. The whole thing is put inside a glass case, to stop air blowing the delicate gold leaf around. The piece of copper goes through insulation in the top of the glass case, so that any charge on the gold leaf cannot escape.

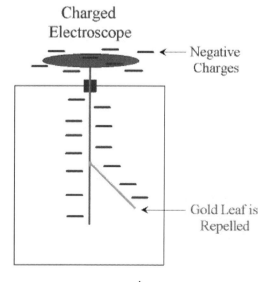

Charge can be transferred to the electroscope by wiping the charged object across the cap. The charge flows over the conducting copper and gold, and the gold leaf rises as it is repelled by having the same charge as the copper.

Electric fields

An electric field is a region in which an electric charge experiences a force. An electric field exists around all electrical charges. The direction of the field is shown by a line of force and these lines show the direction of the force on a positive charge at a given point. The lines, therefore, go from positive to negative.

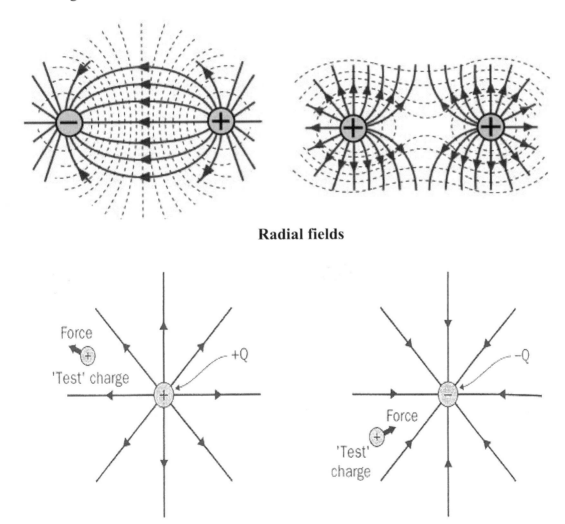

Radial fields

Uniform fields

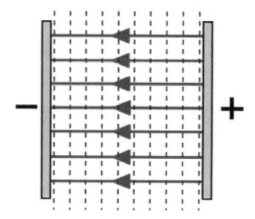

Charge Distribution

When a conductor is charged the charges do not always spread equally over its surface. With a round shape, they are evenly spread but with a pointed shape the charges are always concentrated around the point.

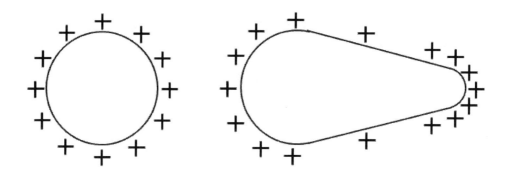

The charge distribution on a conductor fallows the rules below:
- The excess charge lies only at the surface of the conductor.
- The electric field is zero within the solid part of the conductor.
- The electric field at the surface of the conductor is perpendicular to the surface.
- Charge accumulates, and the field is strongest, on pointy parts of the conductor.

To explain why the conductor charges distribution, follow the rules above.

Imagine a negatively charged conductor; in other words, a conductor with an excess of electrons. The excess electrons repel each other, so they want to get as far away from each other as possible. To do this they move to the surface of the conductor.

They also distribute themselves so the electric field inside the conductor is zero. If the field wasn't zero, any electrons that are free to move, would. There are plenty of free electrons inside the conductor and they don't move, so the field must be zero. A similar argument explains why the field at the surface of the conductor is perpendicular to the surface. If it wasn't, there would be a component of the field along the surface. A charge experiencing that field would move along the surface in response to that field, which is inconsistent with the conductor being in equilibrium.

Why does charge pile up at the pointy ends of a conductor? Consider two conductors, one in the shape of a circle and one in the shape of a line. Charges are distributed uniformly along both conductors. With the circular shape, each charge has no net force on it, because there is the same amount of charge on either side of it and it is uniformly distributed. The circular conductor is in equilibrium, as far as its charge distribution is concerned.

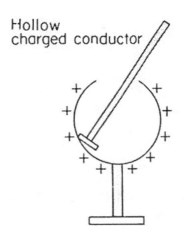

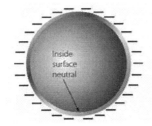

With the line, on the other hand, a uniform distribution does not correspond to equilibrium. If you look at the second charge from the left on the line, for example, there is just one charge to its left and several on the right. This charge would experience a force to the left, pushing it down towards the end. For charge distributed along a line, the equilibrium distribution would look more like this:

The charge accumulates at the pointy ends because that balances the forces on each charge.

Dangers and uses of static electricity

Dangers

When charge jumps across an air gap, it causes a spark. The spark can ignite flammable liquid vapours and powders in pipes.

Care must be taken to avoid sparks when putting fuel in cars or aircraft. The fuel itself is an insulator and charge can be transferred as it flows through a pipe, if the pipe is also an insulator. As the nozzle of the pipe is brought close to the fuel tank, a spark can jump between the two igniting the fuel. The spark can be avoided if the pipe nozzle is made to conduct by connecting an earthing strap to it and so any charge can be safely conducted away. An earthing strap connects the pipe to the ground. In addition, a cable can connect the pipe to the fuel tank, so that there can be no difference in charge between them.

Uses

Electrostatic charge is used in paint spraying, inkjet printers, photocopiers and the removal of pollution from industrial chimneys.

Paint Spraying

The paint is sprayed onto the car bodies and the process is made more efficient by using an electrostatic charge. The paint spray goes past a high voltage positive needle as it leaves the spray gun and the tiny droplets of paint pick up a positive charge. The car body is then given a high voltage negative charge which attracts the positively charged paint droplets. This is good for two reasons.

Firstly, the paint droplets spread out more as they leave the gun. This happens because they all get the same positive charge and so they all repel each other. This is better than coming straight out of the gun as the paint will cover a wider area more evenly.

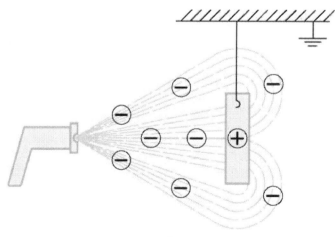

Secondly, the paint droplets are attracted to the negative metal car body, and so less paint will be wasted on the floor or the walls of the paint shop.

Inkjet Printer

An inkjet printer uses electrostatic charge to direct the ink to the correct place on the page. Coloured ink is passed through a very small hole which separates the ink into many tiny droplets. The tiny droplets are given an electrostatic charge. The direction in which the charged ink droplets move can be controlled by electrically charged metal plates. A voltage on the plates means that the charged ink droplets will be attracted to one plate and repelled by the other. This is very similar to an "electron gun" or "cathode ray oscilloscope" where an electron beam is directed to a particular place on a screen.

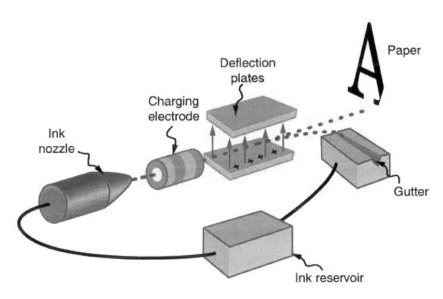

By controlling the voltage on the plates, a particular ink drop can be precisely positioned on the paper.

Photocopier

A photocopier uses electrostatic charge to produce a copy. The original (the page you want copied) is placed onto a sheet of glass.

An image of this page is projected onto a positively charged drum. The drum has a coating which conducts electricity when light falls on it. The parts of the drum which are lit by the projected image lose their electrostatic charge when they start to conduct.

A black powder (called toner) is negatively charged. The toner is attracted to the positively charged parts of the drum.

The drum rotates and rolls against a piece of copier paper. The toner is transferred from the drum to the paper making a black and white image of the original.

Finally, the paper is heated which make the toner stick to it. This is called "fixing" the image. When you use a photocopier, you can feel that the copier paper is still warm

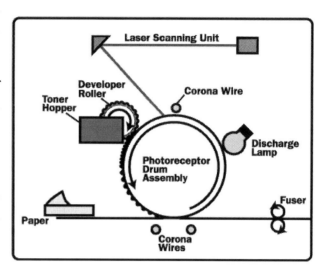

Industrial Chimneys

Pollution from industrial chimneys can be reduced by using electrostatic charge. As well as the waste gases from burning coal (CO_2, SO_2), the chimney contains many small particles of unburnt fuel. The chimney has a high voltage negative grid across it and this gives the small particles a negative charge as they go past.

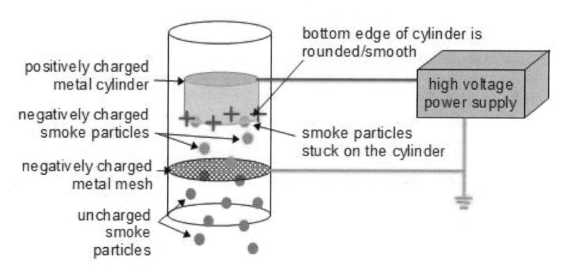

Further up the chimney, there are positively charged plates which attract the negatively charged particles.

The particles of pollution build up on the plates until they are heavy enough to fall down into containers. The containers and the plates are cleaned periodically.

In this way, much of the smoky pollution is removed from the chimney before it can get out into the atmosphere.

The lightning conductor

To protect buildings from lightning, we use a lightning conductor. It is a long, pointed iron rod to the side of the building with its lower end buried in the earth.

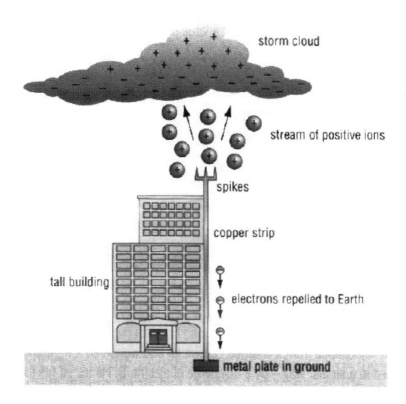

When a negatively charged thunder-cloud passes overhead, it acts inductively on the conductor, charging the points positively and the earthed plate negatively. The negative charge on the plate is immediately dissipated into the surrounding earth. At the same time point action occurs at the spikes. Negative ions are attracted to the spikes and become discharged by giving up their electrons. These electrons then pass down the conductor and escape to earth. The most important part of the action is, however, the upward stream of positive ions. These spread out and form what is called a space charge, which has the effect of reducing the powerful electric forces existing between the cloud and the building. Under these conditions lightning will not normally strike a building, but if it should do so the discharge passes harmlessly to earth through the thick copper conductor.

Without the protection of a lightning conductor, the lightning usually strikes the highest point, generally a chimney, and the current to earth from passes to earth through the path of least resistance. Considerable heat is generated by the passage of the current, and masonry tends to plate split open through the sudden expansion of steam from the moisture contained in it. Sometimes the current has been known to find a path through soot inside a chimney, and to set it on fire

Chapter 2

Electricity

Electric Current

Electric current is the rate of flow of electric charge. The direction of current is the direction of conventional current is the direction of the positive charge.

The unit of electric charge is coulomb. 1 coulomb = 6.2×10^{18} electrons.

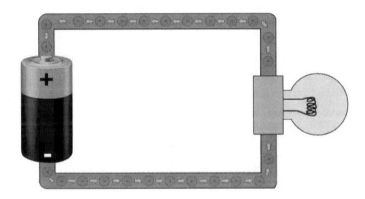

The unit of electric current is ampere or Amp, 1 Amp = 1 coulomb per second.

$$Current = \frac{Charge}{Time}$$

$$I = \frac{Q}{t}$$

Where I is current, Q is charge and t is time.

$$Q = It$$

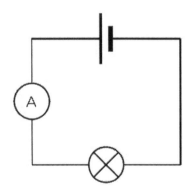

To measure the current through the circuit, we use an ammeter.

The ammeter, shown as a circle with the letter A inside, is always connected in series with a component.

Examples

1   A current of 2 A flows for 10 s, what charge has passed?

$Q = It = 2 \times 10 = 20 \; C$

2   A current of 5 A flows for 2 minutes, what charge has passed?

$$Q = It = 5 \times 2 \times 60 = 600 \; C$$

3   A charge of 20 C passes in 4 s, what is the current?

$$I = \frac{Q}{t} = \frac{20}{4} = 5 \; A$$

Potential difference

The power supply, the cell or battery), gives an amount of energy to each coulomb going around an electric circuit.

1 Volt = 1 joule per coulomb.

Voltage = Energy ÷ Charge.

Energy = Voltage × Charge.

E = V × Q.

A 6 Volt battery gives 6 Joules of energy to each Coulomb going around the circuit. Voltage (called potential difference, or p.d.) is measured using a voltmeter.

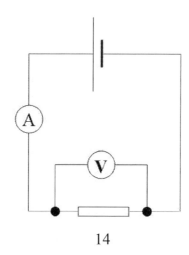

14

The voltmeter, shown as a circle with the letter V inside, is always connected in parallel with the component.

Potential difference provided by cells connected in series is the sum of the potential difference of each cell separately. The bigger the potential difference across a component, the bigger the current that flows through it.

The electromotive force or e.m.f of a cell is equal to the energy converted to electrical energy by the cell per unit charge passing through it. Since the e.m.f. of a cell is also measured in volts, the e.m.f. can be described as the total number of joule per coulomb available from the cell.

You can measure the emf of cell or battery by connecting a voltmeter directly to the cell or battery. The emf is different to potential difference when the cell or battery are part of circuit and electrical current flowing through the circuit. The internal resistance of a battery is the reason why emf and potential difference have different values.

Resistance

Resistance is measured in Ohms (symbol Ω). Resistance of a conductor is a measure of its opposition to the flow of charge, electric current.

The ohm is the resistance of a conductor such that, when a potential difference of 1 volt is applied to its ends, a current of 1 ampere is flow through it.

The bigger the resistance, the smaller the current.

Resistance = Voltage ÷ Current

$R = V \div I$
Or $V = I \times R$

To calculate the resistance of a resistor (A resistor converts electrical energy into heat, it is like a little heater).

Firstly, we need to measure the current flowing through the resistor and the voltage across the resistor.

If the ammeter reads 2 A, and the voltmeter reads 6 V,
then $V = I \times R$
$R = V \div I = 6 \div 2$
$\qquad = 3$ Ohms.

For metallic conductor at constant temperature, the current is directly proportional to the voltage across it.

Ohm's law: The current through a metallic at constant temperature is directly proportional to the voltage across the conductor.

The resistance of a pure metal increases with temperature, but the resistance of certain other conducting materials, e.g., carbon decreases with temperature.

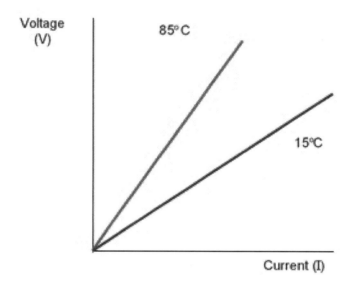

There are three factors that affect the resistance of wire:
- the temperature
- the cross-sectional area and the length the wire. Higher cross-sectional area, the lower the resistance. The longer the wire, the larger the resistance
- the material from which the specimen is made.

The resistance R of a conductor is inversely proportional to its cross-sectional area A.

$$R \propto \frac{1}{A}$$

The resistance R of a conductor is directly proportional to its length L.

$$R \propto L$$

We could combine the two relation ships

$$Resistance\ (R) = \frac{\rho L}{A}$$

ρ is the resistivity, L is length and A is the cross-sectional area.

Resistivity is the resistance of a 1m length and 1 m² of cross-sectional area of a substance. The unit of resistivity is Ω m

Example
4. What is the resistance of the following?
(a) a lamp that draws 2A from a 12V supply

$$R = \frac{V}{I} = \frac{12}{2} = 6\,\Omega$$

(b) a kettle that draws 4A from a 240V supply

$$R = \frac{V}{I} = \frac{240}{4} = 60\,\Omega$$

Electrical Power

Power is measured in watts. Power is an amount of energy supplied in a certain time.

1 watt = 1 joule per second.

Power = Energy ÷ Time.   P = E ÷ t

Power = Voltage × Current

$$P = V \times I$$

And   Energy = Voltage x Current x Time,

$$E = V \times I \times t.$$

Using $V = IR$

$$P = I^2 R$$

Using $I = \frac{V}{R}$, $P = \frac{V^2}{R}$

Example
5. Calculate the power in each of the following cases:

17

(a) a 12 V car battery supplying 50 A;

$$P = V \times I = 12 \times 50 = 600\ W$$

(b) a current of 6 A flowing through a 100 Ω resistor;

$$P = I^2 R = 6^2 \times 100 = 3600\ W$$

(c) a heater of resistance 40 Ω connected to a 240 V supply;

$$P = \frac{V^2}{R} = \frac{240^2}{40} = 1440\ W$$

(d) a discharge of 0.04 C from a pd. of 500000 V in 5 milliseconds.

$$I = \frac{Q}{t} = \frac{0.04}{5 \times 10^{-3}} = 8\ A$$

$$P = V \times I = 500000 \times 8 = 4000000\ W$$

Current/p.d. characteristics

The characteristic of a component is a graph of current against p.d. for the component for a range of values within the component's operating limits. Since some components behave differently when the current through them is in the reverse direction, it is important to measure p.d. and current when the current is in both forward and reverse directions. A typical circuit for obtaining the characteristic is shown in below.

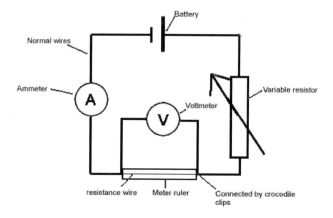

Ohmic conductor

A straight line through the origin is obtained, showing that Ohm's law is obeyed; since the gradient is constant the resistance is constant, for both directions of current flow.

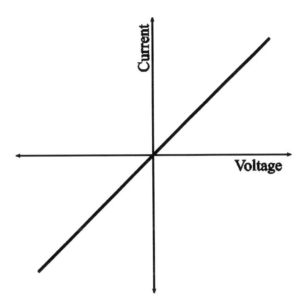

Filament lamp

The curve shows that resistance increases as current increases. This is due to the rise in temperature of the filament, caused by the heating effect of the current.

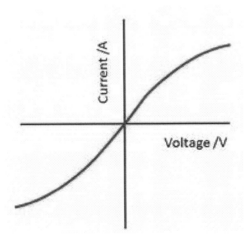

Diode

The diode will allow electricity to pass through it in one direction only. The circuit symbol is like an arrow pointing to a bar. Electricity can only pass in the direction in which the arrow points.

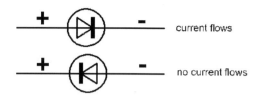

current flows

no current flows

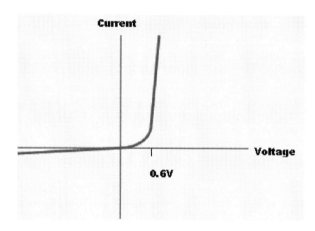

The diode is mainly used in circuits with alternating current.

Light Dependant Resistor

As the name suggests, a light dependant resistor (LDR) is a component whose resistance changes when the amount of light falling on it (called the light intensity) changes. All you need to remember is that the resistance goes down as the amount of light goes up.

Resistance decreases as light intensity increases, light is low, dark is high (resistance).

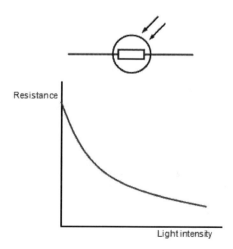

The LDR can be used in a circuit to automatically switch lights on at night

Thermistor

For most components, the resistance rises as the temperature rises. A thermistor is a special type of resistor which has been deliberately manufactured so that its resistance decreases as its temperature rises. A plot of resistance against temperature is given below.

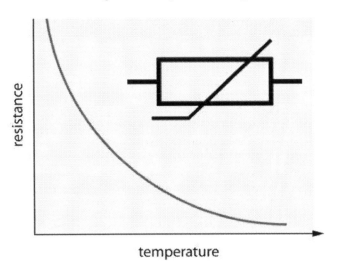

The thermistor can be used in a circuit which senses a temperature change, for example a thermostat to keep the temperature constant, or an alarm if the temperature gets too high or too low (for fire alarms, commercial freezers etc.).

Example
6. A student investigated how the current flowing through component **X** changes with the voltage across it. The diagram shows the circuit used.

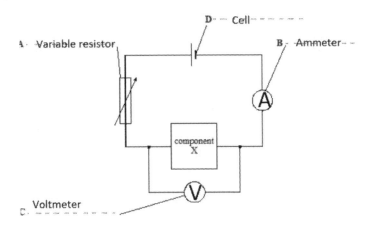

(a) On the diagram, use words or phrases from the list to label parts **A**, **B**, **C** and **D**.

ammeter   **cell**   **switch**   **variable resistor**   **voltmeter**

(b) The table shows the results obtained for component **X**.

VOLTAGE (V)	−0.4	-0.2	0.0	0.2	0.4	0.5	0.6	0.8	1.0
CURRENT (mA)	0	0	0	0	1	4	10	30	50

(i)   Draw a graph of current against voltage.

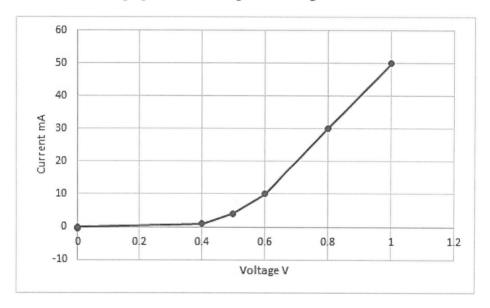

(ii)   Name component X

............Diode..

Series Circuit

When components are connected one following another in a ring, the components are said to be in series with each other and the circuit is called a series circuit.

Current in a Series Circuit

The current in a series circuit is the same everywhere.

22

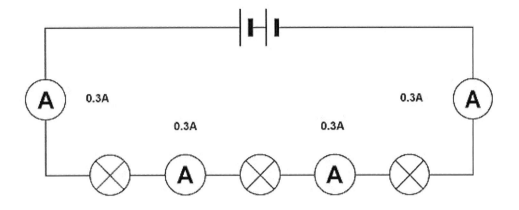

An ammeter placed anywhere in a series circuit always gives the same reading.

In the circuit above, $I_1 = I_2 = I_3 = I_4 = 0.3$ A

Voltage in a Series Circuit
1. The voltage for each component depends on its resistance.
To calculate the voltages below, we need to know the total resistance of the circuit, and the current flowing through it.

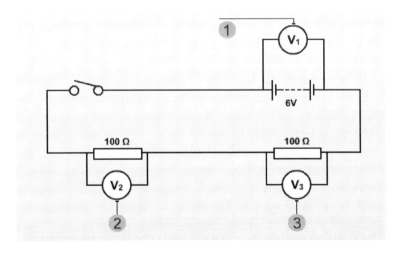

2. The voltage for all components adds up to the supply voltage (from the cell or battery).

$V_1 = V_2 + V_3$

The supply voltage is shared between the components.

Resistance in a Series Circuit

You can calculate the total resistance of a series circuit by adding up the resistance of each component.

$R_{total} = R_1 + R_2 + R_3$

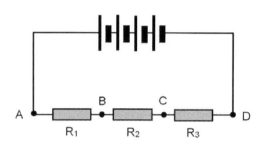

Example
Calculate the total resistance in the circuit above, if $R_1 = 10\ \Omega$, $R_2 = 5\ \Omega$ and $R_3 = 20\ \Omega$

$R_{total} = 10 + 5 + 20$
$\quad\quad = 35$ Ohms

Parallel Circuit

The current in a parallel circuit depends on the resistance of the branch. The total current flowing into the branches is equal to the total current flowing out of the branches.

$I_t = I_1 + I_2 + I_3$

The sum of total current flowing towards a junction in on electric circuit is equal to the sum of total of the current flowing away the junction.

Current in a parallel circuit

The current at A_2 flowing through the 2 Ohm resistor can be found using $V = I \times R$

If the supply voltage is 12 Volts,

$I = V \div R$

$\quad = 12 \div 60$

$= 0.2$ Amps.

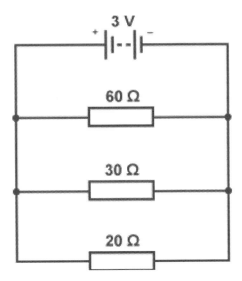

You would get the same answer for the 60 Ohm resistor, whether the other resistors are connected in the circuit.

For parallel circuits, each component behaves as if it is connected independently to the cell and is unaware of the other components.

The current through 30 Ω is $I_2 = 0.4$ A,

The current through 20 Ω is $I_3 = 0.6$ A

$I_t = I_1 + I_2 + I_3$

$= 0.2 + 0.4 + 0.6$

$= 1.2$ Amps.

The general formula for current in parallel circuit is

$I_{Total} = I_1 + I_2 + I_3$

Voltage in a Parallel Circuit

The voltage in a parallel circuit is the same for all branches.

25

$V_1 = V_2 = V_3.$

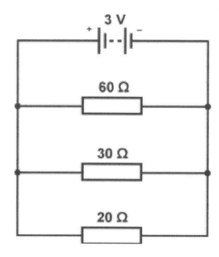

2. The voltage for each branch is the same as the supply voltage.

$$V_1 \; = \; V_2 \; = \; V_3 = \; V_{sup}$$

Using

$$I_{total} \; = \; I_1 + \; I_2 + \; I_3$$

$$\frac{V_{total}}{R_{total}} = \frac{V_1}{R_1} + \frac{V_2}{R_2} + \frac{V_3}{R_{31}}$$

$$\frac{1}{R_T} = \frac{1}{R_1} + \frac{1}{R_2} + \frac{1}{R_3}$$

Putting more resistors in the parallel circuit decreases the total resistance because the electricity has additional branches to flow along and so the total current flowing increases.

Cells in Series

Total voltage = voltage of cell 1 + voltage of cell 2+ voltage of cell 3+ voltage of cell 4 = 6 V

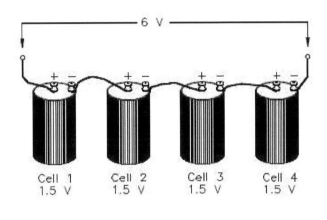

Cells in parallel

Total voltage = voltage of cell 1 = voltage of cell 2 = voltage of cell 3 = 1.5 V

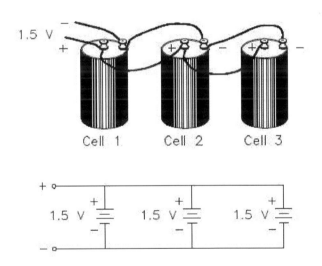

Examples

7. What are the restrictions to Ohms Law?

At constant temperature, the current through a metallic conductor is directly proportional to applied potential difference.

8. A battery is made of four cells, each of 1.5 V and negligible internal resistance. It is connected to three resistors, each of 4 □, in series as shown in the circuit below.

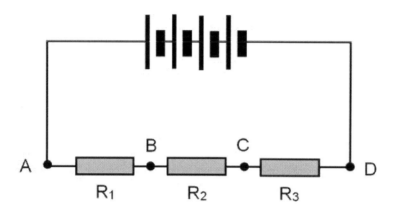

Find:
(a) the total resistance of the three resistors

$$\frac{1}{R_T} = \frac{1}{R_1} + \frac{1}{R_2} + \frac{1}{R_3} = \frac{1}{4} + \frac{1}{4} + \frac{1}{4} = \frac{3}{4}$$

$$R_T = \frac{4}{3} \ \Omega$$

(b) the current flowing in the circuit

Total voltage = 1.5 + 1.5 + 1.5 + 1.5 = 6 V

$$I = \frac{6}{\frac{4}{3}} = \frac{18}{4} = 4.5 \ A$$

(c) the potential difference across R₁

V = 1.5 V

(d) the potential at B;

V = 1.5 V

(e) the potential at C

V = 3 V

(f) the power dissipated in one of the resistors;

$$P = I^2R = (\frac{4}{3})^2 \times 4 = 7.11\,W$$

(g) the current that flows in the circuit if one of the cells is reversed.

Total voltage $= 1.5 + 1.5 + 1.5 = 4.5$ V

$$I = \frac{4.5}{\frac{4}{3}} = 3.37\,A$$

9. The two graphs in the diagram show a specimen of metal wire at two different temperatures.
(a) calculate the resistance of the wire at each temperature
(b) which graph shows the higher temperature?
(c) does the material disobey Ohm's Law? Explain your answer.

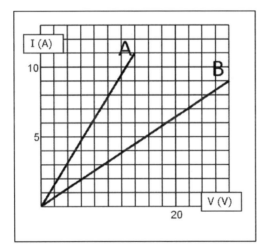

a)

From the graph above, $resistance = \frac{1}{gradient}$

Gradient of line A = 8/5 = 1.6

Resistance of A = 0.625 Ω

Gradient of B = 4/6 = 0.66

Resistance of B = 1.5 Ω

b) The resistance of a metallic conductor increases with temperature. B has higher temperature.

29

c) The materials obey ohm's law. The current through a conductor is proportional to applied voltage.

Chapter 3

Mains Electricity

Energy Transmission

The current and power requirements for circuits used in previous chapter, are small. The current used was battery generated. A battery generates direct current only. direct current is a steady current; it does not change in size or direction with time.

Most mains electricity devices require higher current and power. Millions of watts needed for modern life.
The energy lost in a power cable is given by the formula: Power loss = I^2R. As you can see the power loss depends mainly on electrical current.

To calculating the power loss in a cable, when transferring 1000000 W.

If the resistance of cable is 1 Ω/km.

This power can be transferred as 1000 A and 1000 V

Power loss = $1000^2 \times 1 = 1000000$ W lost. All the power is lost in first km of the cable.

Or

Current 10 Amps and voltage = 100000 volts.

Power loss = $10^2 \times 1 = 100$ W lost. Better Choice, only 100 W per km

This is a large saving of power. For this reason, electricity is transmitted at low current and high voltage. To keep the power loss as small as possible, the transmitted voltage is very high. Electricity generated in a power station at 11 kV is stepped up to 250 kV for transmission across large distances.

However, we can't generate 100000 volts directly and we can't use this type voltage at home. We need to alternating current for transferring electricity long distances, power grid links all power stations to homes and factories.

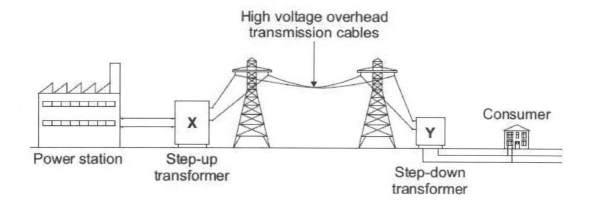

Alternating current

With alternating current, the electrons first start to flow in one direction until the current reaches a maximum value, then the current slows down and stops.

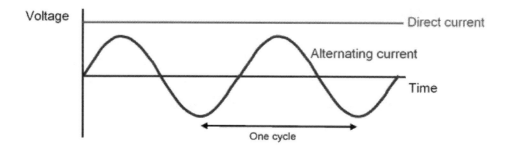

The electrons then start to flow in the opposite direction until the current reaches the same maximum value (but it is now given a minus sign to show it is in the opposite direction), then the current again slows down and stops.

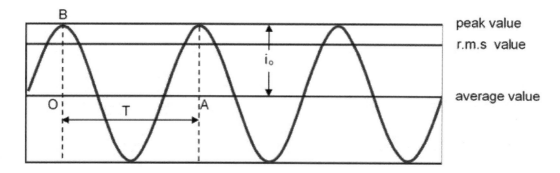

The number of cycles in one second, frequency.

Mains electricity in the UK is supplied at 50 Hz, the effective value of voltage is 240 V while the peak value is 340 V.

The mains electricity supply has three wires. They are called Live, Neutral and Earth and each wire has its own colour. Live is Brown, Neutral is Blue, Earth is Green and Yellow stripes.

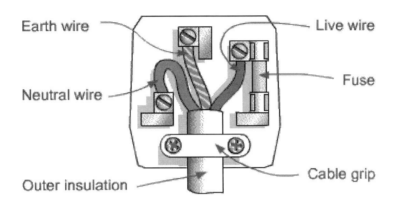

The Live wire is connected directly to the generators of the electricity supply company.

The Neutral wire returns the electricity to the generator after it has passed through the appliance, to complete the circuit. It is actually an earth wire connected to Sub Power Station. In a complete circuit, it carries the same electricity as the Live wire.

The Earth wire usually carries no electricity, it is there as a safety device. If something in the appliance goes wrong, or it is wired incorrectly, then the Earth wire carries the same electricity as the Live wire.

Safety measures

Insulation
Any metal is a conductor. Any non-metal is an insulator, with the exception of graphite which conducts electricity because of its unusual molecular structure.

The wires which conduct electricity are made of a copper metal, which is an excellent conductor. The insulator which covers the wires is a polymer called PVC (often just called "plastic").

Double Insulation

Some appliances are double insulated. These appliances only need Live and Neutral wires, they do not need an Earth wire. An appliance which is double insulated has the whole of the inside contained in plastic, underneath an outer casing.

If anything goes wrong with the appliance, no Live conductor can touch the outer casing because of the insulating plastic. Appliances which are double insulated include electric drills and hairdryers.

Earthing

If the outer casing of an appliance is a conductor, then it can be made safe by Earthing. The Earth wire usually carries no electricity; it is connected to the metal case on the inside of the appliance.

If something goes wrong inside the appliance and the Live wire touches the metal case, then the Earth wire acts like a Neutral wire and completes the circuit for the electricity. A very large current suddenly flows because the metal case has little resistance. This large current will blows the fuse in the plug and disconnects the appliance from the power supply.

Fuses

A fuse is a short thin piece of wire with a low melting temperature, which becomes hot and melts as soon as the current through it exceeds its rated value. The fuse has a rating printed on the outside in amps.

If the fuse rating is 5 amps, then a current greater than 5 amps will blow the fuse. The correct fuse to use is a fuse with current rating just above the current required for the appliances.

To calculate the current required in appliances, we use the formula below

Current = Power ÷ voltage
Amp   watt   volt

10. Find the correct fuse to use in the plug of a hair dryer if the power rating of the hair dryer is 1000 W.

First we need to calculate the current using
Current = Power ÷ Voltage
Then, using

The mains voltage = 240 V
The Current = 1000 ÷ 240 = 4.17 amps. The fuse to use is 5 amps or 5 A

Rectification

For heating and lighting, a.c. is just as good as d.c; but for some uses d.c. is needed. Televisions, radios, battery chargers and electroplating apparatus need d.c. It is therefore useful to be able to convert a.c. into d.c. This can be done using diode.

A diode is a device that allows electricity to flow through it in one direction only.

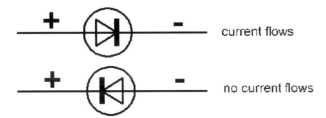

current flows

no current flows

So, if a.c. is applied to the diode, only half of it gets through. You can see how the positive or the negative part of the a.c. cycle can be allowed through simply by turning the diode round.

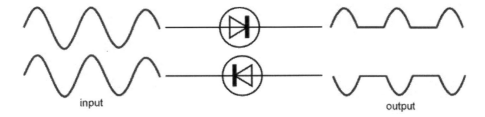

input   output

This type of output is known as half wave rectification. Although the current is not steady, it is now only flows in one direction.

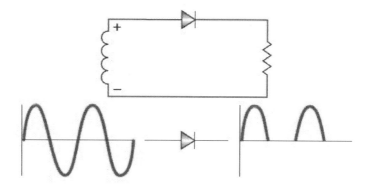

If a capacitor is added to the circuit as shown below, then the output voltage is smoothed. In half wave rectification only half the a.c. cycle is used, the other half being blocked by the diode. By using the circuit below, both half cycles are used.

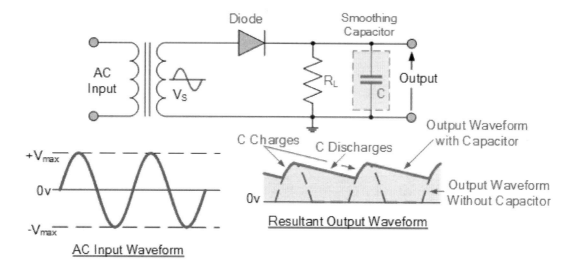

Full wave rectification and the device producing it is called a bridge rectifier, figure below.

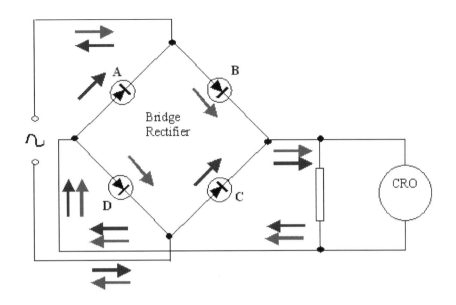

Examples

11. The diagram below shows an electric mains plug.

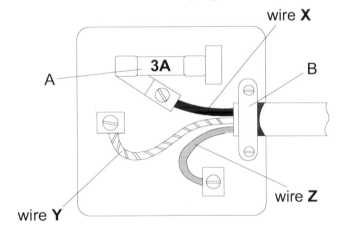

(a) Name the parts of the plug labelled **A** and **B**.

- **A** Fuse..
- **B** Cable Grip

(b) Name the colour of each of the wires **X, Y** and **Z.**

- X - brown/red
- Y - green + yellow/green
- Z - blue/black

(c) Name a suitable material for the case of the plug.

.

Plastic .

(d)　　Electric fires have three wires connected in the plug. One is the live wire to feed electric current in, another is the neutral (return) wire.

(i)　　What is the third wire called?

...earth wire ...

(ii)　　Why is it important that the third wire is also connected?
..... metal appliance needs earthing wire..........

(e)　　The diagram below shows a badly wired mains plug.

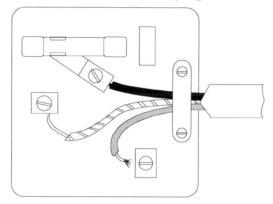

Look at the plug carefully. What **four** changes should be made to make the plug safe?
1. .... cut less insulation on earth;...........................

2. .... fit fuse properly;...

3. .... neutral wire needs connecting.........................

4. .... cable grip needs to be an outer cable.................

Chapter 4

Magnets

A magnet has two poles, called North and South. A magnetic field is a region around the magnet where magnetic materials experience a force. Magnetic materials or ferromagnetic materials are iron, nickel and cobalt. The shape of the magnetic field around the magnet is shown by lines. Arrows on the lines point away from North and towards South to show the direction of the magnetic field.

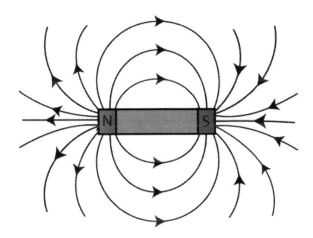

The forces between North and South poles are like the forces between electrostatic charges. Unlike poles attract, like poles repel.

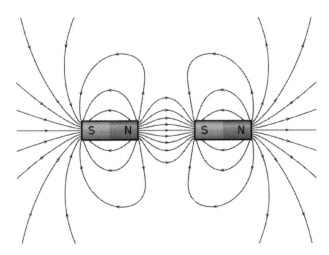

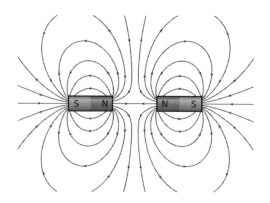

Electromagnets

When a current flow through a conductor, it produces a magnetic field. The shape of the magnetic field depends on the shape of the conductor.

The magnetic field around a straight wire is circular, at right angles to the wire. You can work out the direction of the field using your right clenched fist. Point your thumb upwards in the same direction as the current. The direction of the field is the same direction in which your fingers curl.

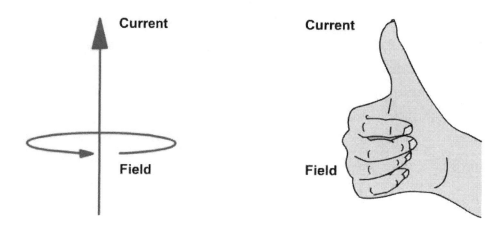

Reversing the direction of the current will reverse the magnetic field direction. The magnetic field around a straight wire is not very strong. A strong field can be made by coiling the wire around a piece of soft iron. This electromagnet is sometimes called a solenoid.

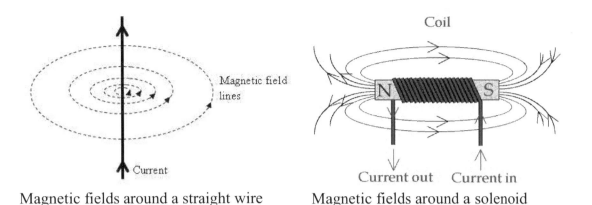

Magnetic fields around a straight wire   Magnetic fields around a solenoid

The shape of the magnetic field is the same as a bar magnet. The soft iron inside the coil makes the magnetic field stronger because it becomes a magnet itself when the current is flowing. Soft iron loses magnetism as soon as the current turn zero. In this way, the electromagnet can be switched on and off by turning the electricity on and off. Steel forms a permanent magnet.

- The strength of the magnetic field around the coil can be increased by
- Using a soft iron core (core means middle bit).
- Using more turns of wire on the coil.
- Using a bigger current.

Reversing the direction of the current will reverse the magnetic field direction.

The magnitude of the magnetic force, on the current carrying wire, can be calculated using the formula

$$F = BIl \sin \theta$$

Where B is the magnetic field strength, I is the electric current, l is the length of wire inside the field and θ is the angle between the field direction and the current.
If θ is 90°, then we could use the formula $F = B \, I \, l$.

Magnetic field strength or magnetic flux density (B) is defined as the force acting per unit current (1A) in a wire of unit length (1 m) which is perpendicular to the field.

Magnetic field strength (B) is defined as the force acting per unit current in a wire of unit length which is perpendicular to the field.

The unit of magnetic field strength is tesla (T).

A magnetic field has a flux density of 1 tesla, if a wire of length of 1 metre carrying a current of 1 ampere and perpendicular to the field experiences a force of 1 newton, in a direction which is perpendicular to both the field and the current.

Magnetic flux is the product of the average magnetic field times the perpendicular area that it penetrates.

$$\text{Magnetic flux } (\Phi) = \text{Magnetic flux density } (B) \times \text{Area } (A)$$

Magnetic flux (Φ) is measured in webers (Wb).

Force on individual charge moving in a magnetic field

using the formula

$$F = B\,I\,l$$

the current can be written using the formula

$$I = \frac{nq}{t}$$

$$F = B\frac{nq}{t}l$$

$$F = Bnq\frac{l}{t}$$

$$F = Bnqv$$

for a single charge

$$F = Bqv \quad \text{for } B \perp v$$

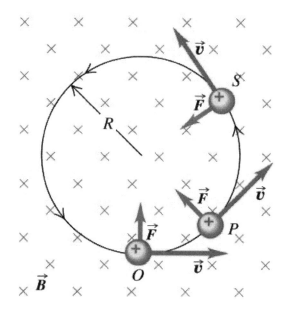

$$F = Bqv\,\sin\theta$$

where θ is the angle between the velocity and the magnetic field.

The above equation applies for any moving, charged particle in a magnetic field. The is no force on the charged particle when it is stationary or if it is moving parallel to the field.

The motor effects

If a wire carrying current was placed in a magnetic field, then there was a force on the wire. The maximum force occurs when the current and the field are at right-angles to each other. The motion is then at right angles to both the field and the current. The bigger the current and the stronger the magnetic field, the greater the force on the wire and the faster it will move.

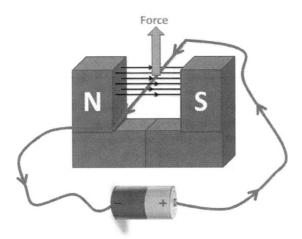

Fleming's Left-Hand Rule is used to predict the movement or direction of force.

Fleming's Left-Hand Rule: If the thumb, first finger and second finger of the left hand are placed at right angles to each other then, diagram right: The First finger represent direction of the Field. The second finger represent the direction of current. The thumb represents the Motion.

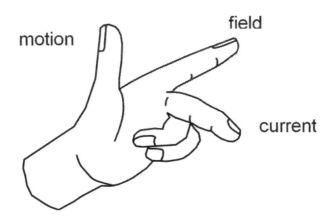

The catapult effects

The catapult effect shows the force on a wire in a magnetic field when current flows through the wire.

The diagrams show a uniform, the field of a wire, and the result of putting the wire uniform field together. It is this third field that is called the catapult field. You can see that the magnetic lines of force are close together near the wire so forcing it upwards. It is rather like the effect of a stretched rubber sheet on an object put on it. If the current direction is reversed the wire will be forced downwards.

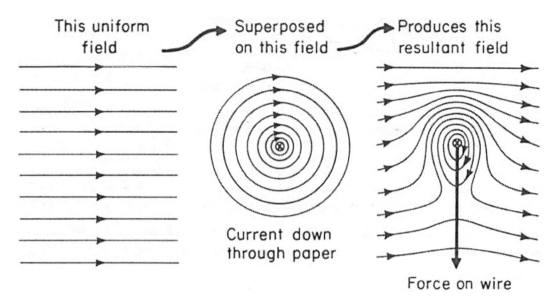

This uniform field → Superposed on this field → Produces this resultant field

Current down through paper

Force on wire

If a coil of wire carrying a current is in a magnetic field, then the way the current flows along one side of the coil will be opposite to the way it flows along the other side.

This means that one side of the coil will be pushed upwards and the other side pushed downwards and so the coil will twist. This rotation of the coil is the basis of all electric meters and motors. With more turns of wire on the coil the twisting force will be greater.

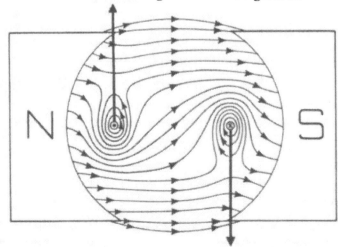

Electric motor

When a wire carrying a current is in a magnetic field, there is a force on it at right angles to the field. A coil in a magnetic field experiences an equal, but opposite force on its two sides, and coil will rotate. A motor consists of a coil, magnet, brushes for dc motor or slip rings for ac motor to connect the coil to power supply.

DC Motors

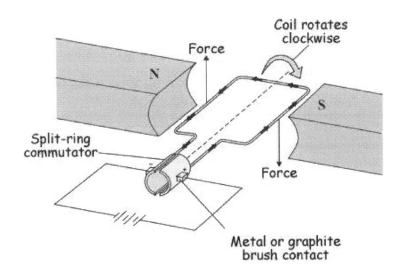

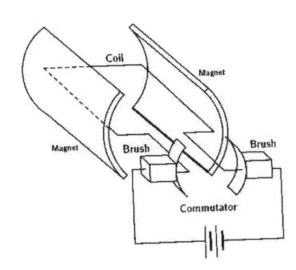

AC Motors

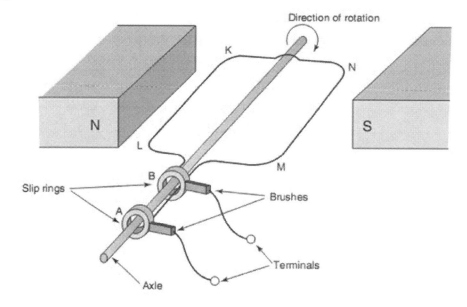

To make the motor turn faster we can:
(a) increase the current
(b) replace the magnets with more powerful ones
(c) push the magnets closer to the coil
(d) put an iron centre piece into the coil
(e) adding more sets of coils around the central core

Electromagnetic induction

When a magnet is moved towards a wire or coil or inside a coil, cutting through the magnetic field lines, an electrical potential difference is induced across the ends of the wire. If the wire is part of a complete circuit, this causes an induced current to flow. This can be shown by connecting the coil to a very sensitive ammeter called a galvanometer.

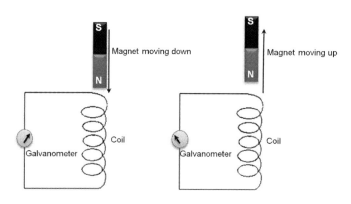

The same effect occurs in a stationary wire in a changing magnetic field. It does not matter if the wire is moved near to a magnet or a magnet is moved near a wire. A stationary wire in a magnetic field which is not changing will not have a current induced in it.

The size of the induced current can be made bigger by:
1. Using a stronger magnet.
2. Moving the magnet at a faster speed.
3. Using more turns of wire on the coil.

The direction of the current can be reversed by:
1. Moving the magnet in the opposite direction.
2. Reverse the polarity of a magnet.

The effect of inducing a current in a coil by moving a magnet inside it is used in generation of electricity in power stations.

Generator

A simple generator is similar to an electric motor. With a motor, we put electrical energy in and get rotational energy out. With a generator we put rotational energy in and get electrical energy out. An a.c generator is shown in Figure below.

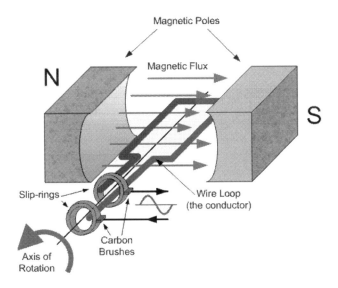

As the coil rotates between the poles of the magnet, the sides of the coil cut through the magnetic field and so a current flow in the coil. The current flows out from both sides of the coil through the slip rings. As one side of the coil cuts down through the field, the output from that side will be positive and as it goes up it will be negative; an ac. output is produced.

The maximum output voltage will be when the coil is parallel to the field. This happens because the coil is cutting the field lines at the greatest rate at this point.

The d.c. generator is like the ac generator. Version, but there are one or two important differences.

There is still a coil that rotates between the poles of a magnet but this time the two ends of the coil are connected to a split ring a half circle of metal that is in contact with the stationary brushes. If you look at the diagram you can see how this arrangement will produce d.c.

As the coil rotates the side of it that is cutting downwards through the field is always in contact with brush 1. That means that brush 1 is always positive. In the same way the side of the coil that is going up is in contact with brush 2.

The device that ensures that the two brushes always have the same polarity is called a commutator.

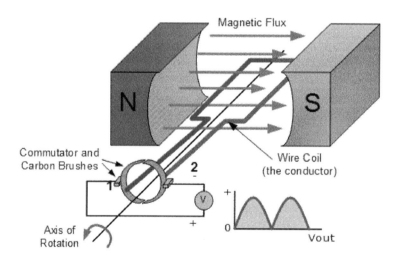

The output of the a.c. generator is shown in the Figure below. The output is not steady but is always in the same direction.

As with the ac. generator the maximum output voltage occurs when the coil is horizontal and is cutting the field at right angles and at maximum rate.

If the generator is turned faster, both the frequency and the amplitude of the wave increase.

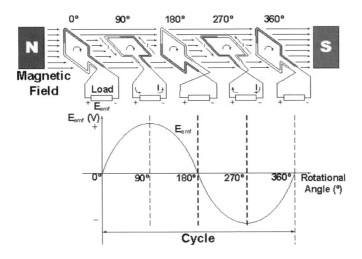

Transformer

A transformer is made from two coils, one on each side of a soft iron core.

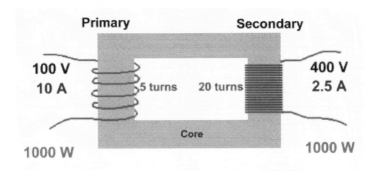

There are two types of transformers:

- Step up where is voltage increased, diagram above. In a step-up transformer, the number of turns in primary are less than the turns in the secondary coil. Having more turns in the secondary coil makes a larger induced voltage in the secondary coil.

- Step down transformer, diagram below. In a step-down transformer, the number of turns in a primary coil are greater than the turns in the secondary coil. Having less turns in the secondary coil makes a small induced voltage in the secondary coil.

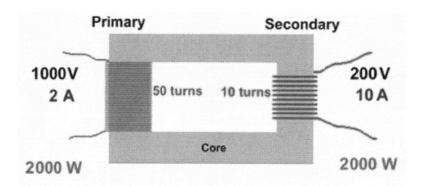

Alternating current is passed through the primary coil which creates a changing magnetic field in the iron core. The changing magnetic field then induces alternating current of the same frequency in the secondary coil.

If the secondary coil has twice as many turns of wire then the output voltage will be twice the input voltage.

$$\frac{Secondary\ voltage\ (V_s)}{Primary\ voltage\ (V_p)} = \frac{Secondary\ turns\ (N_s)}{Primary\ turns\ (N_p)}$$

$$\frac{V_s}{V_p} = \frac{N_s}{N_p}$$

There are two points to remember.
1. Transformers only work with alternating current only. Using direct current will create a magnetic field in the core, but it will not be a changing magnetic field and so no voltage will be induced in the secondary coil.

2. Using a step-up transformer to increase the voltage does not give you something for nothing. As the voltage goes up, the current goes down by the same proportion.

The power equation shows that the overall power remains the same, $P = V \times I$

In reality, the power output is always less than the power input because the changing magnetic field in the core creates currents, eddy currents, which heat the core. This heat is then lost to the environment, it is wasted energy.

Examples

12. A transformer with a primary coil of 2000 turns and a secondary coil of 20 turns has 240 V connected to its primary. What is the output voltage?

V = 240 [20/1200] =240 × 1/10 = 24V

13. What is the ratio of the primary turns to the secondary turns for a transformer that has an input of 20000 V and an output of 400000 V?

N_p/N_s = 20 000/400 000 = 1:20.

Examples

14. (a) An appliance in a house has a transformer. The transformer is used to reduce the voltage to the level needed by the appliance.

The diagram shows the transformer.

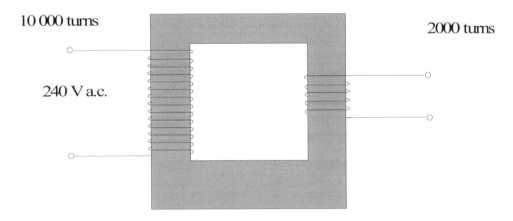

10 000 turns

2000 turns

240 V a.c.

(i) Name the material used for the core of the transformer.
.........................Iron.....................

(ii) The transformer has 10 000 turns on the input side and 2000 turns on the output side. If the mains voltage of 240 volts is applied to the input, calculate the output voltage

$$\frac{V_s}{V_p} = \frac{N_s}{N_p}$$
$$\frac{V_s}{240} = \frac{2000}{10000}$$

Vs = 48 V

(b) Explain, in terms of magnetic fields, how a transformer works.

The changing in the current in primary coil causes changing in magnetic field in core which links to secondary coil which induces an emf in secondary voltage.

(c) A 12 V car battery is connected to the input leads of the transformer. It is hoped to reduce the voltage to 2.4 V in order to run a small motor. When the output voltage is measured it is found to be zero. Explain why the output voltage is zero.
The current from the battery does not change and magnetic field produced by the current does not changing. Therefore, not magnetic flux linage and no electromagnetic induction

(d) A power line supplies electric power to a school via a transformer.

The input voltage of the transformer is 415 V. The transformer changes this to 240 V for use in the school. The power input to the transformer is 48 kW.

The transformer may be assumed to be 100% efficient.

(i) Calculate the current which the transformer supplies to the school.

$$P = IV$$

$$48000 = I \times 240$$

$$I = 200 \text{ A}$$

(ii) The power taken from the National Grid remains constant at 48 kW.

Calculate the electrical energy which is supplied to the school in 1 hour.

$$E = P \times t = 48000 \times 3600 = 172800000 \, J$$

Chapter 5

Nuclear Physics

Atomic Structure

Everything is made of atoms. All atoms have a nucleus. The nucleus of an atom contains protons and neutrons. Protons and neutrons are sometimes called nucleons. All atoms have electrons.

For any atom, the number of protons is the same as the number of electrons. If an atom loses or gains electrons, it is called an ion.

This is a picture of a sodium atom. It has 6 protons, 6 electrons and 6 neutrons.

Each proton has an relative electrical charge of +1. Each electron has an relative electrical charge of -1. The neutron has no charge (it is neutral).

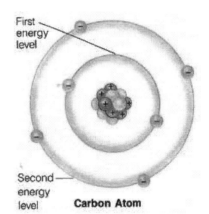

$$relative\ charge = \frac{charge\ of\ particle}{charge\ of\ proton}$$

The charge of proton is 1.6×10^{-19} C

An atom has the same number of protons and electrons so the overall charge is zero (it is neutral).

The mass of an atom is almost equal to the mass of the nucleons it contains. However, as the masses of the atoms and their nucleons are very small when expressed in kilograms, we use a more convenient unit for the masses of the atoms or the masses of nucleons.

1 atomic mass unit = 1 u = $\frac{1}{12}$ of the mass of the nuclide of carbon-12 $^{12}_{6}C$

1 u = 1.66×10^{-27} kg

The mass of 1 mole of $^{12}_{6}C$ is 12 g or 0.012 kg.

$$The\ mass\ of\ 1\ atom = \frac{mass\ of\ 1\ mole}{N_A}$$

Where N_A is Avogadro number = 6.02205×10^{23}

$$mass\ of\ 1\ atom\ of\ carbon = \frac{0.012}{6.02205 \times 10^{-25}} = 1.992676912 \times 10^{-25}$$

$$1\ u = \frac{1}{12} \times 1.99267612 \times 10^{-27}$$

An electron has a relative mass 1÷2000 u

The electrons, although tiny, take up most of the space of an atom. This means that most of the space of an atom contains hardly any mass. It is mostly empty space with nearly all the mass centred at the nucleus.

Nuclear Notation

Standard nuclear notation shows the chemical symbol, the mass number and the atomic number of the isotope.

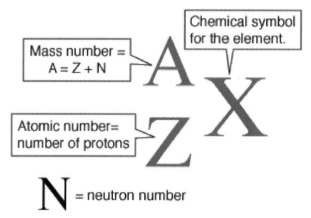

Plum Pudding model

In 1897, J.J. Thomson, discovered the electron, a negatively charged particle, more than two thousand times lighter than a hydrogen atom. Thomson originally believed that the hydrogen atom must be made up of more than two thousand electrons, to account for its mass.

An atom made of thousands of electrons would have a very high negative electric charge. This was not observed, as atoms are usually uncharged.

In 1906, Thomson suggested that atoms contained far fewer electrons, a number roughly equal to the atomic number.

This is only one electron in the case of hydrogen, far fewer than the thousands originally suggested. These electrons must have been balanced by some sort of positive charge.

The distribution of charge and mass in the atom was unknown. Thomson proposed a 'plum pudding' model, with positive and negative charge filling a sphere only one ten billionth of a metre across.

Rutherford and Marsden's Scattering Experiment

Rutherford and Marsden fired very fast a-particles into a very thin piece of gold sheet (called gold foil).

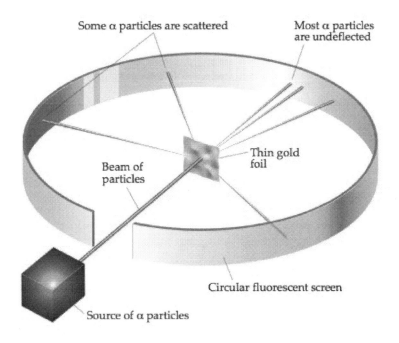

Some α particles are scattered

Most α particles are undeflected

Thin gold foil

Beam of particles

Circular fluorescent screen

Source of α particles

The foil was only a few atoms thick and most of the α-particles went straight through it to the detector.

When the detector was moved around the foil they were surprised to find that a small number of α-particles seemed to have been scattered in all directions.

Some of the α-particles even came back towards the emitter.

Rutherford and Marsden suggested a structure for the atom which would account for the scattering of α-particles

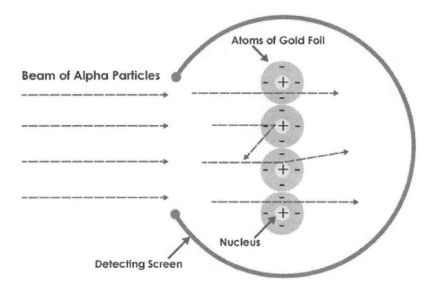

From the results of the scattering experiment on gold foil, Rutherford and Marsden drew the following conclusions.

1. Since most of the α-particles went straight through the foil, most of the space taken up by the atoms must be empty.

2. Since some of the positively charged α-particles were scattered back towards the emitter, they must have been repelled by a positive part (nucleus) of the atom.

3. Since the α-particles were very fast moving, the positive nucleus of the atom must have a lot of mass to be able to stop the a-particles moving forward and repel them back again.

Their model of the atom has a positively charged nucleus which contains the most of mass and electrons orbiting the nucleus, which have almost no mass but take up most of the space.

This is the model of atomic structure which we use today.

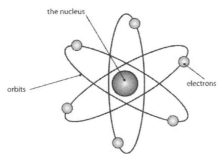

The α-particles travel straight through the electron shells without changing direction.

The red circles represent the positive nucleus. If the α-particle gets close to the positive nucleus it is repelled and changes its direction.

The closer the α-particle gets to the positive nucleus, the more it changes its direction.

If the α-particle goes straight towards the positive nucleus, it is repelled back towards the emitter.

This accounts for the scattering of the α-particles from the gold foil.

Bohr Model of the Atom

Although Rutherford's model of the atom was completely consistent with the results of the alpha-particle scattering experiments, there was considerable opposition to it on theoretical grounds. An orbiting electron is constantly changing its direction and therefore is accelerating. It has been proving that a charged particle accelerating, it emits electromagnetic radiation. orbiting electrons, therefore, could be expected to emit radiation continuously. This is not possible, for if an electron were to emit radiation, it would have to do so at the expense of its own energy and therefore, it would slow down and spiral into the nucleus, in which case the atom could cease to exist.

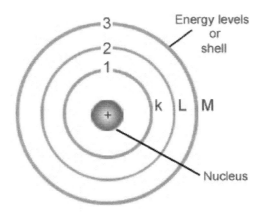

Bohr assumed that each electron moves in a circular orbit which is centred on the nucleus, the necessary centripetal force being provided by electrostatic force of attraction between the positively charged nucleus and the negatively charged electron. On this between basis, he was able to show that the energy of an orbiting electron depends on the radius of its orbit.

Bohr made two proposals:

- Electrons can have only certain values of energy, called energy levels. Therefore, electrons could only occupy certain orbits. Electrons can remain these orbits indefinitely without emitting any energy. Therefore, these energy levels are called stationary states.

- An electron can jump from an orbit in which its energy is E_2, say, to one which is closer to the nucleus and of lower energy, E_1 say. In doing so, the electron gives up the energy difference of the two levels by emitting an electromagnetic wave whose frequency, f, is given by

$$E_2 - E_1 = hf$$

Where is Planck's constant, h = 6.63×10^{-34} Js

Bohr model is that it predicts, to a high degree accuracy, the wavelengths emitted by atomic hydrogen. However, it could not predict accurately the wavelength emitted from other atoms.

Isotopes

Isotopes are particles which have the same position in the Periodic Table, that is, they are atoms of the same chemical element, but their nucleon numbers are different. Isotopes of an element have nuclei with the same number of protons but different numbers of neutrons.

Neon, for instance, has three isotopes with nucleon numbers of 20, 21 and 22, corresponding respectively to 10, 11 and 12 neutrons in the nucleus. The most common isotopes of uranium are uranium-235 and uranium-238 (143 and 146 neutrons respectively.)

It is important to realise that since the number of electrons is identical for all isotopes of the same element, the chemical properties of isotopes of the same element are identical. Since the structure of the nuclei are different. However, their nuclear properties will be different and, since their relative atomic masses are different, some of their physical properties are different as well. For example, the boiling point of 'heavy water' (water containing the isotope of hydrogen with a neutron in the nucleus) is 104 ^{0}C.

Example: the isotopes of carbon. The element is determined by the atomic number 6. Carbon-12 is the common isotope, with carbon-13 as another stable isotope which makes up about 1%. Carbon 14 is radioactive and the basis for carbon dating.

$$^{12}_{6}C, \ ^{13}_{6}C, \ ^{14}_{6}C$$

Radioactivity

In 1896, Henri Becquerel, who was Professor of Physics at the University of Paris, discovered that uranium salts could fog a photographic plate even if the plate was covered. He deduced that the salts were emitting some form of radiation that could pass through the wrapping. He also found that this radiation could ionise a gas, causing a charged electroscope to discharge.

This phenomenon is called radioactivity, or radioactive decay; and the 'radiations' are emitted when an unstable nucleus disintegrates to acquire a more stable state. The disintegration is spontaneous and a random process which gives out heat and most commonly involves the emission of an α-particle or a β-particle. In both α-emission and β-emission the parent nucleus, the emitting nucleus, undergoes a change of atomic number and therefore becomes the nucleus of a different element. This new nucleus is called the daughter nucleus or the decay product.

There are three types of radioactivity, called α (alpha), β (beta) and γ (gamma). A radioactive nucleus will emit either an alpha particle or a beta particle or a gamma ray.

The number of protons is called the atomic number. The number of protons plus neutrons is called the mass number. The mass number is sometimes called the nucleon number.

The unit of activity of a radioactive source is the becquerel (Bq).

1 Bq is one disintegration per second or 1 emission of α, β or γ

Experiments have identified the three types of radiation as:

- Alpha – the two protons and two neutrons (the nucleus of a helium atom)
- Beta – high speed electrons
- Gamma – very short wavelength electromagnetic radiation

Property	Alpha (α)	Beta (β)	Gamma (γ)
Range in air	A few cm	a few tens of cm	metres
Ionising ability	large	small	very small
Stopped by	paper	mm of aluminium	cm of lead
Charge	+2e	-e	0
Mass	8000 m	m	0
Deflection by magnetic field	a little	a lot	none

Speed	<1%c	90% c	c

Where m, is the mass of the electron and c, is the speed of light, 300 000 000 m/s

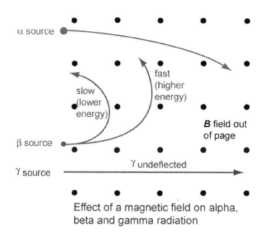

Effect of a magnetic field on alpha, beta and gamma radiation

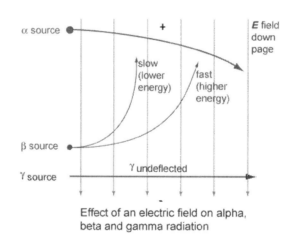

Effect of an electric field on alpha, beta and gamma radiation

Penetrating Ability

The ability of radioactivity to pass through materials is called its penetrating ability.
It depends on the size of the radioactive particle.

The bigger the particle, the more likely it is to collide with the atoms of the material.
The collision will stop the particle going through the material.

α-particles are the biggest and are least able to penetrate a material. Paper will stop them and even in air a-particles only travel for a few centimetres before they are stopped.

60

β-particles are stopped by a few millimetres of aluminium.

γ-rays are the most able to penetrate and will even find their way through metres of concrete.

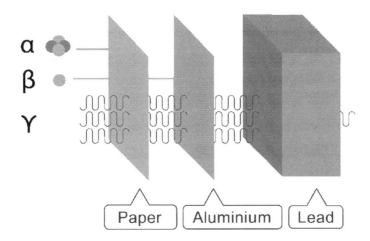

When the particle or ray collides with the material, it can knock an electron off the atom and form an ion.

Penetrating ability is related to ionising ability. The one which is least able to penetrate is the most likely to cause ions.

Ionising Ability

All types of radioactivity form ions. They are called "ionising radiation". When α-particles, β-particles or γ-rays collide with a material, they can knock an electron off an atom in the material and form an ion. Radioactivity can be detected because it forms ions. A smoke detector works because ions are formed around a radioactive source.

The cells of the body may undergo dangerous physical and chemical changes as a result of exposure to radiation. The extent of the damage depends on the nature of the radiation, the part of the body exposed to the radiation, the dose received.

α-particles are absorbed in the dead surface layers of the skin and therefore do not constitute a serious hazard unless their source is taken into the body. γ -rays can penetrate deeply into the body and are a serious hazard.

The energy liberated by radiation within a material is known as the radiation dose and is measured in units known as grays (Gy). A gray is an energy liberation of 1 joule per kilogram of the material.

Different radiations affect the body more than others, each having what is known as a relative biological effectiveness (RBE). Then

effective dose = radiation dose × RBE

The relative biological effectiveness of some radiations are given below.

Radiation	RBS
beta, gamma, X	1
neutrons (slow)	3
neutrons (fast)	10
alpha	10-20
Fission product	20

The unit of effective dose sievert, radiation dose is measured in gray

Alpha α Particles

Rutherford and Royds made a direct identification of the alpha-particle in 1909. There experiment proved that, an α-particle is the nucleus of a helium atom. It consists of 2 protons and 2 neutrons.

It is written ^4_2He or $^4_2\alpha$

An α-particle has by far the most mass of the three types of radiation. It is the most likely to collide with other atoms which means that α-particles have the least penetrating ability and are easily absorbed by paper, skin or a few centimetres of air. Alpha particles are the most ionising of the three types of radiation. Alpha particles are likely to be emitted during the decay of heavy nuclei which have a large number of protons and neutrons

After a radioactive nucleus has emitted an α-particle, the mass number goes down by 4 and the atomic number goes down by 2.

For example, Radium (Ra) becomes Radon (Rn) by emitting an α-particle.

$$^{224}_{88}\text{Ra} \longrightarrow ^{220}_{86}\text{Rn} + ^{4}_{2}\text{He}$$

The nuclear equation is balanced because the mass number on the left of the arrow is equal to the sum of the mass numbers on the right of the arrow, 224 = 220 + 4.

Similarly for the atomic numbers, 88 = 86 + 2.

Radon is itself radioactive and decays by α emission.

$$^{220}_{86}\text{Rn} \longrightarrow ^{4}_{2}\text{He} + \; ?$$

You can work out what the new element is by balancing the equation. 220 = 4 + 116, 86 = 2 + 84.

The element with atomic number 84 is Polonium

$$^{220}_{86}\text{Rn} \longrightarrow ^{4}_{2}\text{He} + ^{216}_{84}\text{Po}$$

Beta β-particles

From measurements of their charge-to-mass ratio, Becquerel showed that beta particles, were in fact electrons. It is often called a high energy electron because it is very fast moving.

A β-particle comes from the nucleus of an atom. It has a charge of -1 and very little mass (only 1 ÷ 1840 as big as a proton).

It is written $^{0}_{-1}\text{e}$ or $^{0}_{-1}\beta$

It is given a mass number of zero because the mass is very small compared to a proton or a neutron. β-particles have more penetrating ability than α-particles but may be absorbed by a few millimetres of aluminium.

After a radioactive nucleus has emitted a β-particle, the mass number stays the same and the atomic number goes up by 1.

A neutron in the nucleus has changed into a proton plus an electron. The proton stays inside the nucleus, but the electron is given out as a β-particle.

For example, Carbon-14 becomes Nitrogen-14 by emitting a β-particle.

$$^{14}_{6}C \rightarrow\ ^{14}_{7}N + ^{0}_{-1}e$$

Or if you went be accurate

$$^{14}_{6}C \rightarrow\ ^{14}_{7}N + ^{0}_{-1}e + ^{0}_{0}\bar{v}$$

Where $\bar{v}$ is called antineutrino.

The nuclear equation is balanced because the mass number on the left of the arrow is equal to the sum of the mass numbers on the right of the arrow, $14 = 14 + 0$. Similarly, for the atomic numbers, $6 = 7 - 1$.

Other examples beta decay

$$^{23}_{12}Mg \longrightarrow\ ^{23}_{11}Na + ^{0}_{+1}e + ^{0}_{0}v$$

This decay produces an antiparticle to an electron, positron, and a neutrino.

Gamma γ-rays

In 1914, Rutherford and Andrade managed to diffract gamma-rays by a crystal, showing them to be electromagnetic in nature with a wavelength of about 10^{-13} m.

Alpha and beta emission is often accompanied by gamma emission. After the alpha or beta emission, the daughter nucleus is left in an excited state. At some point this excited nucleus will decay by emission of a gamma ray.

A γ-ray has no mass and no charge.

It is written $^{0}_{0}\gamma$

Emitting a γ-ray makes no difference to the mass number or the atomic number but will make the nucleus more stable.

It is the least likely to collide with other atoms which means that gamma rays have the most penetrating ability and are not easily absorbed. Many centimetres of lead or a few metres of concrete will absorb most γ-rays but some will still get through.

Gamma rays are the least ionising of the three types of radiation. Gamma rays are likely to be emitted at the same time as α-particles or β-particles but some isotopes only emit γ-rays.

When a radioactive nucleus emits an α-particle or a β-particle the protons and neutrons in the new nucleus may not be in their most stable form. The protons and neutrons can rearrange themselves to become more stable and in this process energy is emitted in the form of gamma rays.

Below are examples of both α and β emitters which give off γ-rays.

$$^{238}_{92}U \longrightarrow {}^{234}_{90}Th + {}^{4}_{2}He + {}^{0}_{0}\gamma$$

$$^{90}_{38}Sr \longrightarrow {}^{90}_{39}Y + {}^{0}_{-1}e + {}^{0}_{0}\gamma$$

Electron Capture

This occurs when an orbital electron is captured by the nucleus. A parent nucleus may capture one of its orbital electrons and emit a neutrino. This is a process which competes with positron emission and has the same effect on the atomic number.

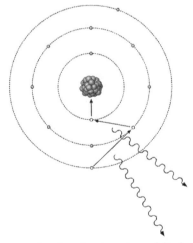

The capture of electrons leads to vacancies in electronic orbitals and these are filled when electrons from outer orbitals occupy them and lose energy in the process.

A typical example of electron capture

$$^{7}_{4}Be + {}^{0}_{-1}e \longrightarrow {}^{7}_{3}Li + \nu$$

Background Radiation

Whenever a radiation detector is switched on, it will always indicate the presence of radioactivity, even if there are no radioactive sources nearby. The detector is measuring the background radiation, which is always present. This background radiation has many sources, including cosmic radiation, which originates outside the Earth, the presence of natural radioactive materials in the rocks around us and a small amount of emissions from the medical, military and industrial applications.

This entire radioactivity is called the background radiation. The level of this radiation (called the background count) is low.

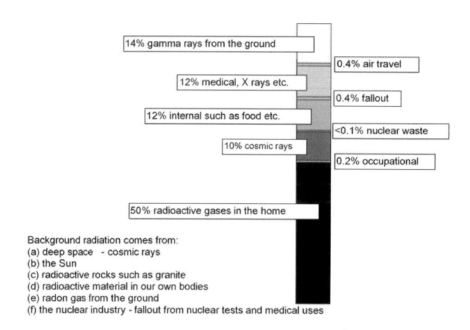

Background radiation comes from:
(a) deep space   - cosmic rays
(b) the Sun
(c) radioactive rocks such as granite
(d) radioactive material in our own bodies
(e) radon gas from the ground
(f) the nuclear industry - fallout from nuclear tests and medical uses

Half-Life

Half-life is the time taken for half of the radioactive nuclei to decay. Or half-life is the time taken for the count rate to fall to half of its original reading.

The following graph shows how the activity of a source (in counts per second) decreases with time.

This means that if we have some material that has a half life of 3 days then after 3 days it will only be half as radioactive as it was at the start. After another 3 days, i.e 6 days after the start, it will only be a quarter as radioactive, one eighth after 9 days and so on.

The half-life depends only on the material of the source and different radioactive isotopes have different half-lives.

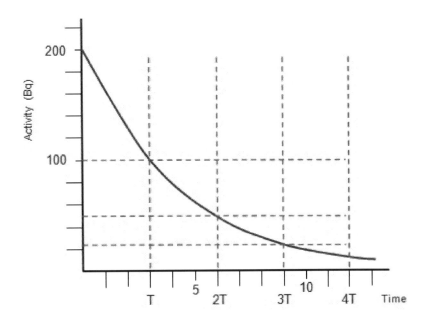

The activity of a sample is directly proportional to the number of radioactive atoms in the sample. We can use the half life to predict the activity of a sample at any time in the future.

$$Activity, A \propto Number\ of\ radioacctive\ atoms, N$$

Since the activity halves every half-life, it will fall to one half after one half life, a quarter after two, an eight after three and so on. A very useful formula for calculating the final:

$$A = \frac{A_0}{2^n}$$

where n is the number of half-lives that have passed.

The original activity is A_0 and the activity after n half-lives have gone by is A.

Uses of Radioactivity

Radioactive dating

Radioactive substances with long half-lives stay around for a very long time. When a particle radioactive nuclide and its decay products become trapped as rock solidifies or a plant or creature dies, they start a very slow radioactive clock. The clock tells us how much time has passed since the radioactive nuclei was trapped. One such clock is the uranium clock, which starts when rocks are formed. At the end of a decay series, uranium atoms form a stable isotope of lead.

A measurement of the fraction of uranium atoms which have decayed into lead atoms tells how old the rock is.

For example, after 4500 million years, the half-life of uranium $^{238}_{92}U$, here are the same number of lead atoms as uranium atoms because, half of uranium atoms have decayed. After another 4500 million years there will be three lead atoms for every one uranium atom.

The carbon-14 clock tells us how long ago something died. Radiation from space converts nitrogen in the atmosphere into the radioactive nuclide of carbon, $^{14}_{6}C$ (or carbon-14).

A very small but constant proportion of carbon dioxide in the atmosphere contains these unstable carbon-14 atoms which decay by ß-emission with a half-life of 5730 years. The other carbon atoms are the stable isotopes $^{12}_{6}C$ and $^{13}_{6}C$. Only about one carbon atom in 10^{12} is radioactive carbon-14. Living plants take in carbon dioxide (containing this small proportion of radioactive carbon-14) as they grow, and animals eat some of the plants. The carbon atoms become trapped in the remains of a plant or animal at the moment of its death. At death, all plants and animals contain, trapped in their tissues and bones; the same proportion of carbon-14, as is always present in the atmosphere. So, at death, a radioactive clock is started as the trapped carbon-14 atoms decay and are not replaced by new ones from the atmosphere. Every 5730 years, the number of carbon-14 atoms left in the fossil remains of plants and animals, halves.

The fraction of $^{14}_{6}C$ to $^{12}_{6}C$ is also half every 5730 years. By measuring the fractional remains of carbon -14 today in fossils and comparing it with the fraction when the clock started ($1/10^{12}$), the length of time, the radioactive clock is running, can be calculated.

Radioactive tracers

If a little radioactive material, is put into a moving liquid, the path of this liquid can be tracked. It is used in testing blood flow, tracking underground streams and following the movement of silt in rivers. In radioactive tracing, two factors affect the choice which materials to use. First, the penetration power and second the half -life. In medical uses for example, material used an isotope of Technetium, ^{99m}Tc.

The ^{99m}Tc isotope is a gamma emitter and has a half-life of 6 hours. Most gamma radiation can pass through the body and has a half- life of 6 hours. It means most radioactive materials will decay in less than two days.

Radiotherapy

Low intensity gamma radiation can damage living cells and cause cancer. High intensity gamma radiation will kill cells. It is used in a technique called radiotherapy to treat cancer by targeting the cancer cells with a beam of radiation and then rotating the source of the beam as shown below.

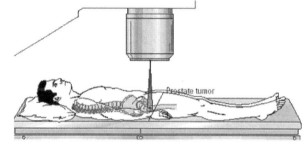

Radiotherapy aims to kill the cancer cells while doing as little damage as possible to healthy normal cells.

Thickness gauge

The amount of radiation which passes through a material can be detected and used to control the thickness of the material. A beta source is put on one side of a sheet of material and a Geiger counter on the other. The amount of beta radiation that gets through the sheet will give you an idea of its thickness.

Smoke alarms

Many houses have a smoke alarm using a weak alpha source. When smoke gets into the detector. the alpha particles cannot get through to the sensor and the alarm goes off.

The radioactive source in a smoke detector is an alpha emitter. The alpha particles pass between the two charged metal plates, causing air particles to ionise. The ions are attracted to the oppositely charged metal plates causing a current to flow.

When smoke enters the smoke detector, the smoke particles near to the radioactive source absorb many of the alpha particles before they can ionise the air between the charged plates. This means a smaller than normal current flows so the alarm sounds.

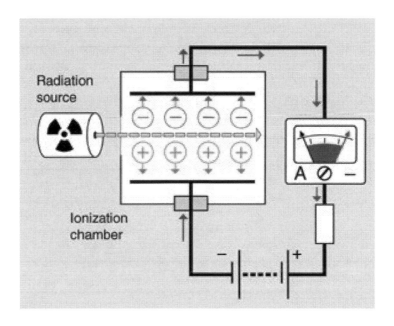

Cracks in castings

A gamma source is placed in a metal casting and a Geiger counter moved over its surface. If there are any cracks in the metal, gamma radiation can get through and be detected.

Sterilisation of food

Bacteria in food can be killed if exposed to gamma radiation.

Biological effects of radioactivity

The exposure to ionising radiation is very dangerous. The danger is due to the absorption of energy from the radiation by tissues of the body. As the body absorbs radiation energy, ions are produced which can change or destroy living cells.

The main risk from α- and ß-radiation comes from inside a person. Since α- and ß-particles do not penetrate very far into the body, the risk from external sources is quite small. α particles have a very short range and can be stopped by a sheet of paper. Their only biological effects are to the surface of the skin.

However, care must be taken to avoid radioactive materials being eaten or inhaled from the air. Therefore, no eating, drinking or smoking is allowed where any radioactive materials are handled, and disposable gloves and protective clothing are worn. Masks are worn in mines where radioactive

70

dust particles are air-borne. X- and γ-rays can be absorbed deep inside the body, they will affect the internal organs of the body due to its high penetrating power. People exposed to external sources of X-radiation and γ-radiation must be protected as much as possible. Most of human exposure to X-ray are made using man made tubes like in hospital's X-ray machine and not natural sources like in electron capture.

People who work with ionising radiation wear a film badge which gives a permanent record of the radiation dose received. The sensitive film is covered with various metal filters through which different kinds of radiation can pass and darken the film behind. The darkness of the film behind the different filters indicates both the amount and type of radiation received. Workers are also checked for radiation contamination by using sensitive radiation monitors before they leave their place of work.

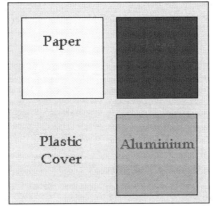

A worker handling radioactive materials may use remote-controlled tools and sit behind a shielding wall made of lead and concrete.

In medical diagnosis, when X-rays are used to produce 'shadow pictures' of bones and internal organs, the radiation dose is kept to a minimum in the following ways:
- The X-ray beam is restricted to expose only the part of the body where the image is required. Lead shutters or 'beam definers' are used to control where the X-rays come out of the X-ray tube.
- Aluminium filters are used to absorb unwanted 'soft' X-rays, which are absorbed by the body rather than pass through to the X-ray plate.
- The exposure time is kept as short as possible.
- Modern systems use an intensifying screen which makes it possible to obtain an X-ray image from a much lower level of radiation.
- The number of X-ray exposures is limited for any patient, but any exposure is to be avoided for unborn babies and young children.

In nuclear reactors, neutron radiation presents special problems. Because neutrons are uncharged, they produce few ions and so have a relatively long range in body tissue. However, because of their large mass, they cause considerable damage when they collide with living cells. A neutron has about the same mass as a hydrogen nucleus, and since the body contains large numbers of hydrogen nuclei in its cells, the neutrons lose a lot of energy and thus the cells are severely damaged. As the neutrons have similar mass to hydrogen atoms, a collision between a neutron and a hydrogen will result in neutron losing its energy to the hydrogen. Neutrons can be stopped using materials containing a large amount of hydrogen atoms such as paraffin wax.

Radiation can cause immediate damage such as radiation burns out but possibly its long-term effects are even more serious. Besides leukaemia, it causes cancer and genetic damage since it affects the rapidly dividing cells in the body, such as those in the liver and the reproductive organs. Radiation can also damage the eye, causing cataracts which destroy its clarity. For these reasons, radioactive sources must always be handled carefully and sensibly.

Nuclear Fission

Nuclear fission is the disintegration of a heavy nucleus into two lighter nuclei. If a massive nucleus like uranium-235 breaks apart, then there will be a net yield of energy because the sum of the masses of the fragments will be less than the mass of the uranium nucleus. If we fire a neutron at this nucleus it becomes unstable and splits.

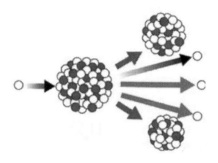

The U-235 nucleus captures the slow neutron and becomes very unstable that a short time later, it splits into two fission fragments. These are the nuclei of lighter elements, containing around 30 to 60 protons (the total number of protons in the fragments must be 92). In addition, several neutrons (typically three) will be ejected at high speeds. A large amount of matter is converted to energy in the process, which appears as kinetic energy of the fission fragments and neutrons. The high speed neutrons are unlikely to cause further fission. After few collisions with uranium nuclei, the speed neutron will small enough for another uranium nucleus to absorb it and split again. As for each This is called a chain reaction. Slowed down neutrons are known as thermal neutrons because their slow speed and low kinetic energy is matched to the thermal (heat) energy of the surrounding material

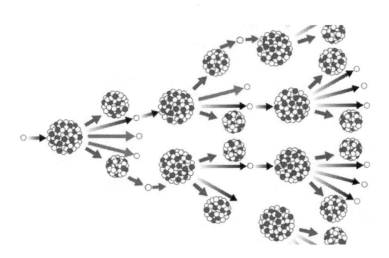

You only get a chain reaction if there is enough uranium 235 and it is the right shape, otherwise too many neutrons will escape from the outside and the reaction will stop. A sphere is an ideal shape, as it has the smallest surface area to its mass. The smallest amount of uranium needed to keep a chain reaction going is called the critical mass.

Nuclear Fission Reactor

The neutrons produced in a chain reaction are moving too fast to cause further fission in U235 nuclei and they have to be slowed down. This is done by graphite or heavy water and these materials are called moderators. As the neutrons collide with atoms of the moderator, they slow down. The control rod, made of boron steel or cadmium, which absorb neutrons, can be raised or lowered into the reactor core to control the rate of the chain reactions. The further into the core a control rod is lowered the more neutrons it will absorb and the more chain reactions it will stop. The control rods are held on electromagnetic clamps so that if there is a dangerous increase in core temperature they can be dropped into the reactor and so shut down the chain reaction.

In a nuclear reactor, the fuel is in the form of hundreds of narrow rods surrounded by the moderator. These fuel rods each contain less than the critical mass of fissionable uranium. Most of the emitted neutrons leave the fuel rod and collide with the atoms of the moderator, slowing down in the process, before reaching the next fuel rod at the right speed to cause further fission reactions. The material used for a moderator has to have a low mass number so that as much as possible of the neutron's kinetic energy is transferred at each collision.

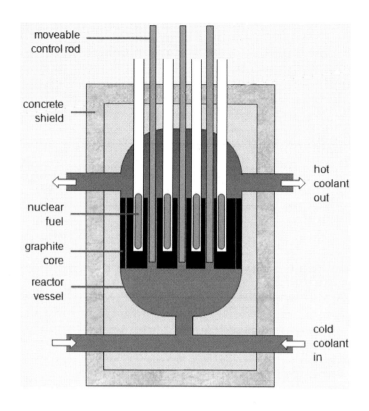

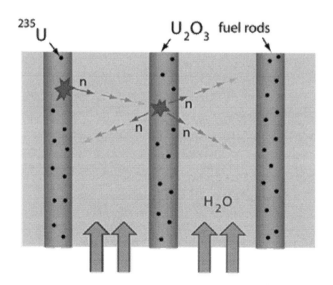

Nuclear Fusion

If light nuclei are forced together, they will fuse with a yield of energy because the mass of the combination will be less than the sum of the masses of the individual nuclei. If the combined nuclear mass is less than that of iron at the peak of the binding energy curve, then the nuclear particles will be more tightly bound than they were in the lighter nuclei, and that decrease in mass comes off in the form of energy according to the Einstein relationship. For elements heavier than iron, fission will yield energy.

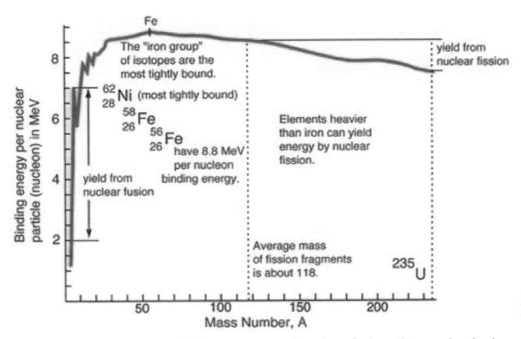

Stars generate their own heat and light by a process of nuclear fusion. Converting hydrogen into helium.

However, the nucleus of a hydrogen atom is a positively charged proton. When two protons approach each other, they will repel each other, since they have the same charge. The protons must be moving extremely fast, if they are to have enough energy to overcome the force of repulsion. The four protons can join together to form helium

Each Helium created will require four hydrogen atoms.

First two of
$$^1_1H + {}^1_1H \rightarrow {}^2_1H + {}^{0}_{+1}\beta + \upsilon$$

And then two,
$$^2_1H + {}^1_1H \rightarrow {}^3_2He + \gamma$$

Finally,

$$^3_2He + {}^3_2He \rightarrow {}^4_2He + {}^1_1H + {}^1_1H$$

75

For potential nuclear energy sources for the Earth, the deuterium-tritium fusion reaction.

First two of

$$_1^2H + {_1^2}H \rightarrow {_1^3}H + {_1^1}H + Energy$$

And finally

$$_1^2H + {_1^3}H \rightarrow {_2^4}H + {_0^1}n + Energy$$

The reason that energy is produced is that the mass of the two deuterium nuclei is slightly greater than the mass of the one helium nucleus. This tiny difference becomes energy. You can work out the amount of energy released by using the famous equation proposed by Albert Einstein:

$$E = mc^2$$

Where c is the speed of light.

Star Formation and Death

Stars are hot bodies of glowing gas that start their life in nebulae. A Nebulae is a giant cloud of gas and dust (mainly hydrogen).

They vary in size, mass and temperature, diameters ranging from 450x smaller to over 1000x larger than that of the Sun. Masses range from a twentieth to over 50 solar masses and surface temperature can range from 3,000 degrees kelvin to over 50,000 degrees kelvin.

The larger its mass, the shorter its life cycle. A star's mass is determined by the amount of matter that is available in its nebula. Over time, the hydrogen gas in the nebula is pulled together by gravity and it begins to spin. As the gas spins faster, it heats up and becomes as a protostar. The extra kinetic energy raises the temperature of the hydrogen and the atoms collide with each other more frequently.

At 3,000 Kelvin, a protostar's core will be hot enough for its atoms to ionise, leaving only positively-charged hydrogen and helium nuclei. Meanwhile, the compression exerted by the surrounding mass continues to increase. If enough mass gathers, the force of gravity exceeds the force of repulsion between the hydrogen nuclei and makes these nuclei "fuse". Fusion turns hydrogen into helium and releases a huge amount of energy as heat and light. The star becomes a main sequence star.

In main sequence stars, the fusion reaction turns hydrogen into helium. Most main sequence stars are stable. They have constant size and temperature. Inside the star, there are two opposing forces. Gravity is the force causing the star to contract. The heat released from fusion causes the star to expand. These opposing forces balance each other, and the size of the star stays almost constant.

The length of time that a star lasts as a main sequence star depends on how big it is. Big stars use up their hydrogen at a much faster rate than small ones. The Sun has been a main sequence star for five billion years. It is expected to last for another five billion years. The Sun is about half way through its main sequence phase.

When the hydrogen in the core begins to run out, the star is no longer generating heat by nuclear fusion in the core. The core becomes unstable and contracts. The outer shell of the star, which is still mostly hydrogen, starts to contract with the core. Eventually, the temperature of shell near the core will be large enough for a fusion reaction to start. The outer shell will expand as result of the heat generated by fusion in inner shell. As the outer shell expands, it cools and glows red. This stage is called red giant. It appears red because the surface of the expanded star has cooled. The rate of expansion continues, and the star expands to produce a red giant, the size of the Earth's orbit.

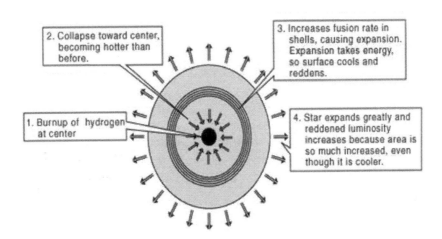

The core is mainly helium. The temperature of the core will continue to rise as the core collapses. Eventually, the temperature core rises enough for the fusion of helium to begin. This stage is called the triple alpha process. Helium is fused to give beryllium and finally carbon. For stars with a mass less than 3 solar masses, this occurs rapidly and is called a helium flash.

Depending on the size of the red giant, it may then become a white dwarf or a supernova.

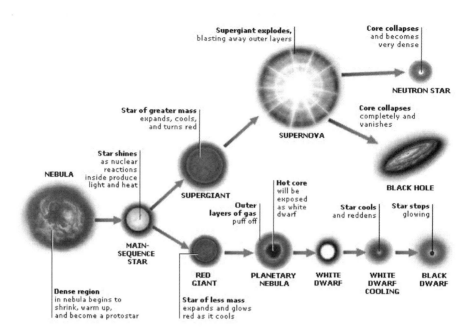

The diagram shows the following labels:

Supergiant explodes, blasting away outer layers

Core collapses and becomes very dense

NEUTRON STAR

Star of greater mass expands, cools, and turns red

Core collapses completely and vanishes

SUPERNOVA

Star shines as nuclear reactions inside produce light and heat

NEBULA

Hot core will be exposed as white dwarf

BLACK HOLE

Outer layers of gas puff off

SUPERGIANT

Star cools and reddens

Star stops glowing

MAIN-SEQUENCE STAR

RED GIANT

PLANETARY NEBULA

WHITE DWARF

WHITE DWARF COOLING

BLACK DWARF

Dense region in nebula begins to shrink, warm up, and become a protostar

Star of less mass expands and glows red as it cools

Dwarf

All stars below a critical value, estimated to be in the range of 6 to 8 solar masses, will finally become white dwarves. That is 90% of all stars in our galaxy. The white dwarf state is the third and final state of star life. It happens after they have exhausted their nuclear fuel.

Near the end of its nuclear burning stage, this type of star expels most of its outer material, creating a planetary nebula. Only the hot core of the star remains. This core becomes a very hot white dwarf. A white dwarf is an extremely dense object. On average, the density of white dwarf is 1 million times bigger than average density of material on earth.

In time, about 40 billion years, the star loses energy, and becomes a black dwarf. A black dwarf can no longer be visible, it is not emitting any light.

Neutron Star and Black Hole

Neutron stars and black holes are among the most exotic objects in the universe. It is the result of a large star becoming highly unstable at the end of its red giant phase. It can contract very rapidly and undergo an explosion called a supernova. During the explosion, the star can become intensely bright for a very short period.

A single supernova can be as bright as all the other stars in the galaxy added together.

The outer part of the star, which may contain a large number of heavy elements, is blown into space and can form the substance of new solar systems. The central core of the star is compressed into a super dense material and forms a neutron star. The core is made of neutrons squashed together and may be one million times as dense as a white dwarf.

If the core of a neutron star is very big then the gravity is so great that the material becomes infinitely squashed. It is now so small that it hardly exists at all. It is now called a black hole.

A black hole is a region of space in which the matter is so compact that nothing can escape from it, not even light; the "surface" of a black hole, inside of which nothing can escape, is called an event horizon. The matter that forms a black hole is crushed out of existence.

In principle, black holes can have any mass; black holes formed by stellar death have at least twice the mass of our Sun. That is the mass after the supernova stage.

Examples

15. The diagram below shows the paths of two alpha particles A and B into and out of a thin piece of metal foil.

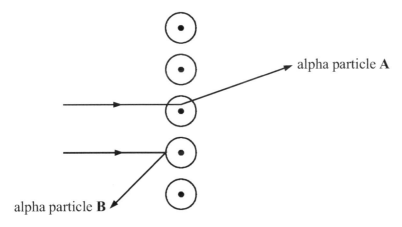

   (a)   The paths of the alpha particles depend on the forces on them in the metal. Describe the model of the atom which is used to explain the paths of alpha particles aimed at thin sheets of metal foil.

   Positively charge nucleus. The nucleus is very small when compared with size of atom. Electrons are negatively charge and orbit the nucleus.

   (b)   Scientists used to believe that atoms were made up of negative charges embedded in a positive 'dough'. This is called the 'plum pudding' model of the atom.

79

The diagram below shows a model of such an atom.

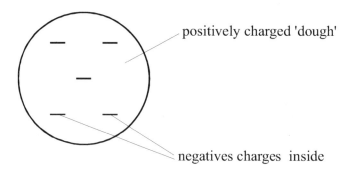

(i)   Explain how the 'plum pudding' model of the atom can explain why alpha particle **A** is deflected through a very small angle.

Positive part of the atom, dough, repels positive alpha particles. The force between the atom and alpha is very small, which results in small change the direction of alpha.

(ii)   Explain why the 'plum pudding' model of the atom can not explain the large deflection of alpha particle **B**.

Large force is needed to produce large deflection as in B. The positive charge in plum pudding spread out and as such the force produced by the positive charge is very small. The positive charge must be concentrated in nucleus

(c)   We now believe that atoms are made up of three types of particles called protons, neutrons and electrons.

Complete the table below to show the relative mass and charge of a neutron and an electron. The relative mass and charge of a proton have already been done for you.

PARTICLE	RELATIVE MASS	RELATIVE CHARGE
proton	1	+1
neutron	1	0
electron	0	-1

(2)

(d)   The diagrams below show the nuclei of four different atoms **A**, **B**, **C** and **D**.

Key: ○ – proton   ● – neutron

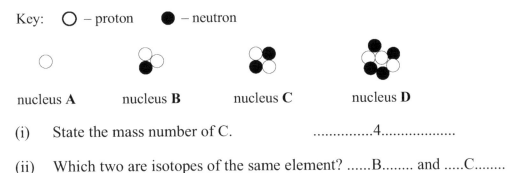

nucleus **A**   nucleus **B**   nucleus **C**   nucleus **D**

(i)   State the mass number of C.   ....4...................

(ii)   Which two are isotopes of the same element? ......B........ and .....C........

Explain your answer.

Both have the same number of protons and different number
of neutrons

16. The diagram shows a film badge worn by people who work with radioactive materials.
The badge has been opened. The badge is used to measure the amount of radiation to
which the workers have been exposed.

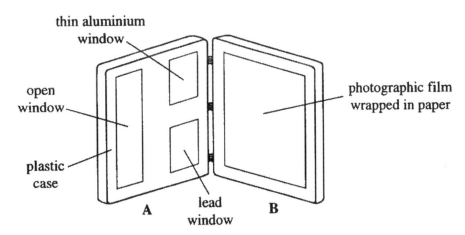

(a)   The detector is a piece of photographic film wrapped in paper inside part **B** of
the badge.
Part **A** has "windows" as shown.

Complete the sentences below.

When the badge is closed

(i)   ......Beta......... radiation and ....Gamma..... radiation can pass through

81

the open

window and affect the film.

(ii) Most of the ....Gamma........ radiation will pass through the lead window and

affect the film.

(b) Other detectors of radiation use a gas which is ionised by the radiation.

(i) Explain what is meant by *ionised*.

Atoms or molecules loss electrons as results of collisions between the electrons and ionizing radiation.

(ii) Write down **one** use of ionising radiation.

.... kill cancer cells ....

(c) Uranium-238 has a very long half-life. It decays via a series of short-lived radioisotopes to produce the stable isotope lead-204.

Explain, in detail, what is meant by:

(i) *half-life*,

The time taken for no. of radioactive nuclei to halve

(ii) *radioisotopes*.

Atoms with unstable nuclei which emit radiation.

(d) The relative proportions of uranium-238 and lead-204 in a sample of igneous rock can be used to date the rock. A rock sample contains three times as many lead atoms as uranium atoms.

(i) What fraction of the original uranium is left in the rock?

(Assume that there was no lead in the original rock.)

..........Two half lives   1/4............................

(ii)   The half-life of uranium-238 is 4500 million years.

Calculate the age of the rock.

2   × 4500 million = 9000 million

17. An experiment to determine the half-life of a radioactive gas using a Geiger-Müller tube and a ratemeter gave the following results:

Time /s	0	20	40	60	80	100	120	140	160
Count/Bq	71	55	43	34	26	20	16	12	10

Plot a graph and estimate the half-life of the gas.

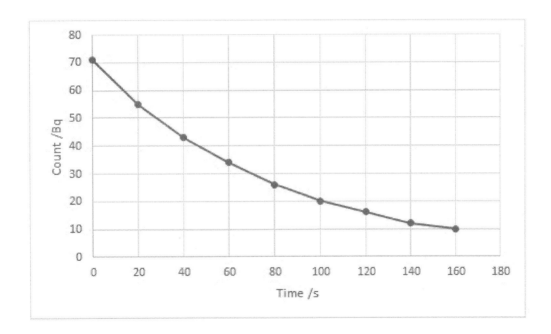

Half life 58 s

Revision Questions

18. What is the current used by a 60 W lamp connected to a 240 V supply?

19. Should a voltmeter have a high or low resistance? Explain your answer.

20. Should an ammeter have a high or low resistance? Explain your answer.

21. Calculate the combined resistance of 2 Ω, 4 Ω and 6 Ω connected (a) in series; (b) in parallel.

22. What is the meaning of electromotive force (e.m.f.)?

23. In the circuit below, what happens when the switch is closed, which lamps light? Calculate the total resistance of the circuit if resistance of each bulb is 200 Ω.

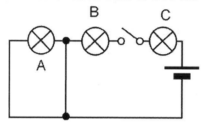

24. In the circuit in below which lamps light when:
(a) S_1 is closed;
(b) S_1 and S_2 are closed?

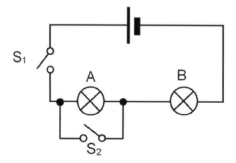

25. What will the in each ammeter in circuits below?
All cells and lamps are identical.

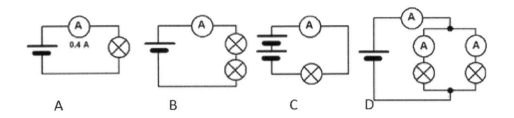

A   B   C   D

26. How many joules of energy are given to 2 C by a 6 V battery?

27. How many joules of energy are used when a current of 100 A flows from a 8 V car battery for 10 s?

28. Which uses more energy per second, a 100 W bulb running at 0.25 A or a 5 W bulb running at 0.25 A?

29. Calculate how much electrical energy is supplied by a 12V battery when:
(a) a charge of 2000C passes through it
(b) a current of 5.5A flows from it for 75s

30. How much energy is drawn from a 12V car battery if it is used to supply 120A for 10s to the starter motor.

31. You have five 1.5V cells. Explain how you would connect them to give:
(a) the highest output potential

(b) a given current for the longest possible time

(c) an output potential of 4.5V

32. 20 identical light bulbs are connected in series across a 240V d.c supply.
(a) what is the p.d across each bulb
(b) what is the potential at the join of the second and third bulbs from the negative terminal?

Voltage across each = 240/20 = 12 V
Assuming bulb1 is connected to 240V potential. The potential between second and third is 216V.

33. Calculate the current through the following resistors:

(a) 4700 Ω connected to 12V
(b) 10kΩ connected to 24V
(c) 2.5MΩ connected to 3V

34. What is the resistance of the following?
(a) a torch bulb that draws 0.25 A from a 12V supply
(b) an immersion heater that draws 10 A from a 240V supply

*35 Two heating coils dissipate heat at the rate of 50 W and 100 W respectively when they are connected in series with a 12 V supply.

(a) What is the resistance of each coil?
(b) What would the total rate of heat dissipation become if they were then connected in series, their resistances remaining constant?

*36 A 12 V, 10W, bulb is connected in series with a 240 V, 60 W, bulb to the 240 V mains. Explain what will happen to both bulbs when the supply is switched on.

37 Two parallel resistances of 8 and 6 Ω are connected to the terminals of a battery consisting of four dry cells, each having an e.m.f. of 1.5 V in series (a) calculate the current through each resistor (b) the total current.

38. (a) The graph below shows how the current in two resistors, A and B, changes as voltage changes.

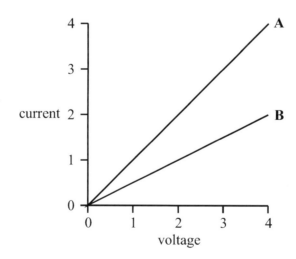

(i) How, if at all, does the resistance of resistor A change as voltage is increased?

(ii) How does the resistance of resistor B compare with that of resistor A?

(b) The diagram shows a battery connected to two resistors.

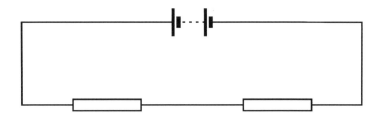

Complete the following sentence about the circuit.

The .... from the battery is shared between the resistors whilst the same .... flows through each one.

(c) In this question all the cells are identical. Each cell has a voltage of 1.5 volts. The diagrams below show three ways of making a battery. In each case two cells are used.
Under each battery write the voltage you would expect the battery to have.

.... volts   .... volts

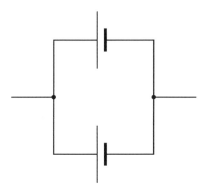

....volts

39. (a) A student is to design an electrical circuit which will indicate when the temperature inside an incubator is 40 °C.

(i) Name a suitable temperature sensor for the student to use.

(ii) Draw the circuit symbol for the temperature sensor you named above.

(b) Before designing the circuit the student measured the resistance of the sensor at different temperatures. The results are shown in the table.

Temperature in °C	Resistance of sensor in ohms
0	3000
10	2000
20	1400
30	1000
40	700
50	500

(i)   Draw a graph of these results.

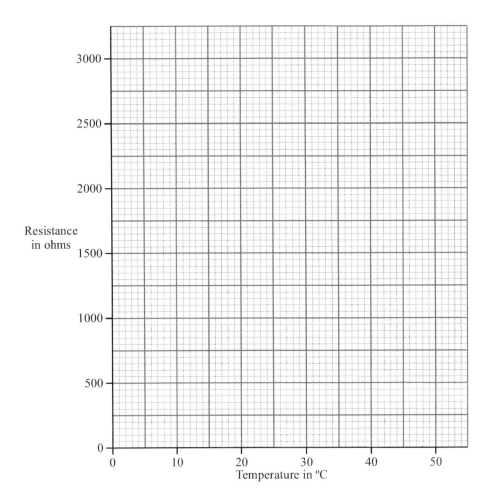

40. (a) The diagram shows the voltage-current graphs for three different electrical components.

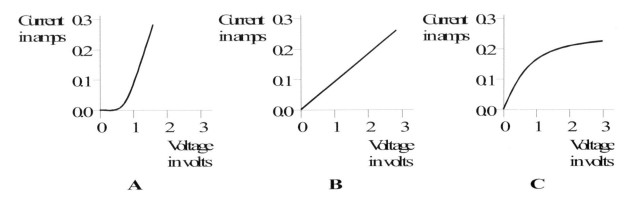

Which one of the components A, B or C could be a 3 volt filament lamp? Explain the reason for your choice.

(b) Using the correct symbols draw a circuit diagram to show how a battery, ammeter and voltmeter can be used to find the resistance of the wire shown.

Thin wire

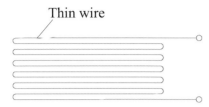

(c) When correctly connected to a 9 volt battery the wire has a current of 0.30 amperes flowing through it.

(i) Give the equation that links current, resistance and voltage.

(ii) Calculate the resistance of the wire. Show clearly how you work out your answer and give the unit.

(iii) When the wire is heated, the current goes down to 0.26 amperes. State how the resistance of the wire has changed.

41.   The information plate on a hair drier is shown.

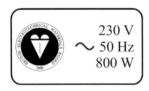

230 V
∿ 50 Hz
800 W

(a) What is the power rating of the hair drier?

(b) (i) Write down the equation which links current, power and voltage.

(ii) Calculate the current in amperes, when the hair drier is being used. Show clearly how you work out your answer.

(iii) Which one of the following fuses, 3A, 5A or 13A, should you use with this hair drier?

(c) The hair drier transfers electrical energy to heat energy and kinetic energy.

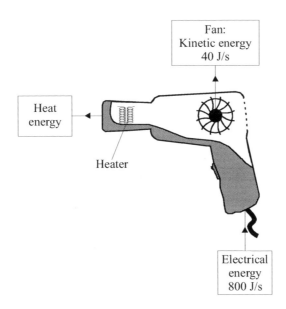

Fan:
Kinetic energy
40 J/s

Heat
energy

Heater

Electrical
energy
800 J/s

Use the following equation to calculate the efficiency of the hair drier in transferring electrical energy into heat energy.

$$\text{efficiency} = \frac{\text{useful energy output}}{\text{total energy input}}$$

42. The drawing shows someone ironing a shirt. The top of the ironing board is covered in a shiny silver-coloured material.

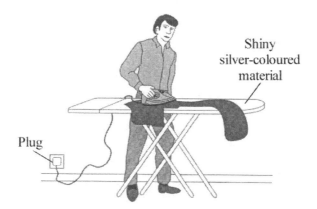

Shiny
silver-coloured
material

Plug

(a) Explain why the shiny silver-coloured material helps to make ironing easier.

(b) The iron must be earthed to make it safe. Which part of the iron is connected to the earth pin of the plug?

Metal soleplate — Plastic part

(c) Name a material that could be used to make the outside case of the plug.

Give a reason for your choice.

43. (a) A steel nail may be magnetised by an electric current. Describe, with the aid of a diagram, how you would do this.

(b)   The diagram below shows a transformer.

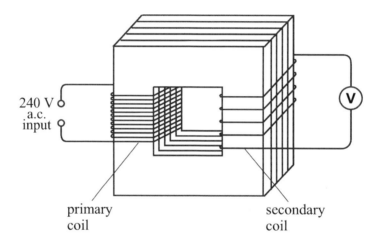

240 V a.c. input

V

primary coil

secondary coil

(i) Name the material used to make the core of the transformer.

(ii) The primary coil has 48 000 turns and the secondary coil 4000 turns. If the input voltage is 240 V a.c., calculate the output voltage.

(iii) Explain how the use of such a transformer could be adapted to transform a low voltage into a higher voltage.

44. The outline diagram below shows part of the National Grid. At **X** the transformer increases the voltage to a very high value. At **Y** the voltage is reduced to 240 V for use by consumers.

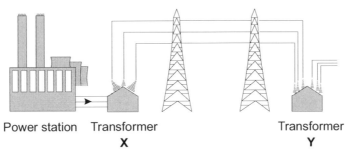

Power station   Transformer
X
     Transformer
Y

(i) The frequency of the mains supply to houses is 50 Hz. Explain what this means.

(ii) At **X** a transformer increases the voltage. What happens to the current as the voltage is increased?

(iii) Why is electrical energy transmitted at very high voltages?

(iv) The transformer at **Y** reduces the voltage before it is supplied to houses. Why is this done?

45. The diagram below shows an electric generator.

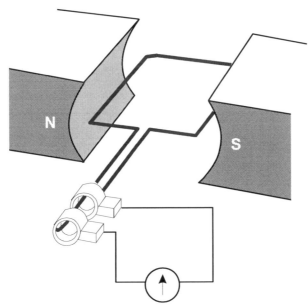

(a) What must be done to the generator to enable it to produce electricity?

(b) Why is a voltage induced in the coil?

(c) Give **four** ways in which the size of the induced voltage could be increased if another generator was built.

46. (a) In the diagram below a magnet, attached to a spring, is free to vibrate in a coil of wire.

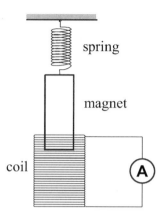

When the magnet is pushed down and released its vibrations rapidly die away.

The magnet is now replaced by an iron bar, the same size and mass as the magnet. When this is pushed down the same distance and released its vibrations take considerably longer to die away.

Explain why the vibrations of the magnet did not last as long as those of the iron bar.

(b)   The diagram below shows a dynamo suitable for use on a cycle.

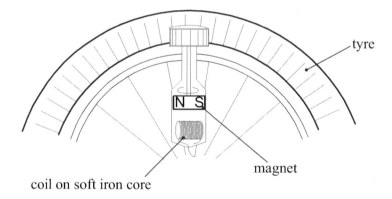

 (i) Explain why a voltage is generated when the dynamo is turned by the tyre.

(ii) Explain why the brightness of the lamp increases as the cyclist goes faster.

(iii) Describe **three** changes you would make to the design of the dynamo if you wanted it to generate a bigger voltage.

47. The diagram shows apparatus used to demonstrate the motor effect. **X** is a short length of bare copper wire resting on two other wires.

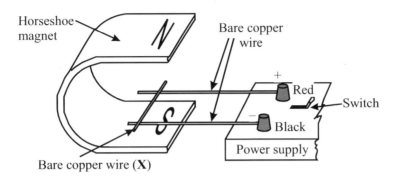

(a)(i) Describe what happens to wire **X** when the current is switched on.

(ii) What difference do you notice if the following changes are made?

(b) The diagram shows a coil placed between the poles of a magnet. The arrows on the sides of the coil itself show the direction of the conventional current.

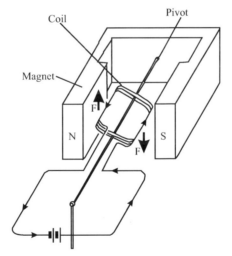

The arrows labelled **F** show the direction of the forces acting on the sides of the coil. Describe the motion of the coil until it comes to rest.

(c) Most electric motors use electromagnets instead of permanent magnets. State three of the features of an electromagnet which control the strength of the magnetic field obtained.

48. The diagram below shows a coil of wire connected to a meter which can measure small currents.

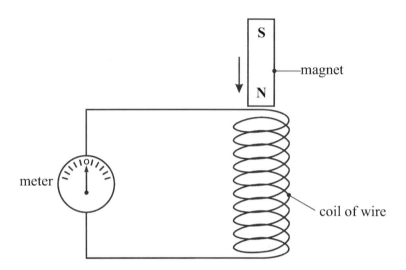

(a) What, if anything, happens to the needle of the meter as the magnet is moved into the coil?

(b) The magnet is now left stationary inside the coil as shown in the diagram below.

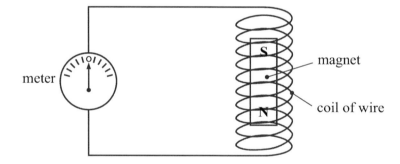

What, if anything, happens to the needle of the meter?

(c) What, if anything, happens to the needle of the meter as the magnet is lifted out of the coil?

49. The diagram below shows a door lock which can be opened from a flat inside a building.

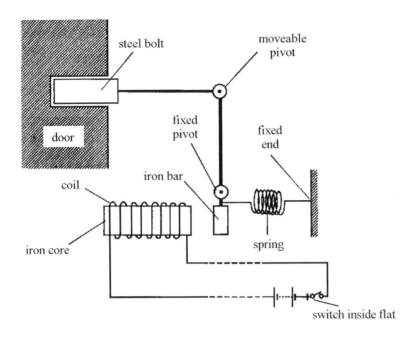

(a) Explain how the door is unlocked when the switch is closed.

(b) State **two** changes which would increase the strength of the electromagnet.

(c)   Why is the spring needed in the lock?

(d) The connections to the coil were accidentally reversed. Would the lock still work?

The iron bar would still be attracted as coil still be magnetised, so still works

50. A patient suffering from cancer of the thyroid gland is given a dose of radioactive iodine 131, with a half-life of 8 days, to combat the disease. He is temporarily radioactive, and his nurses must be changed regularly to protect them. If his radioactivity is initially 4 times the acceptable level, how long is it before the special nursing rota can be dropped?

51. Stars are formed from massive clouds of dust and gases in space.

(a) What force pulls the clouds of dust and gas together to form stars?

(b) Once formed a star can have a stable life for billions of years. Describe the two main forces at work in the star during this period of stability.

(c) What happens to this star once this stable period is over?

(d) Suggest what might then happen to a planet close to this star.

52. (a) The Sun is at the stable stage of its life.

Explain, in terms of the forces acting on the Sun, what this means.

(b) At the end of the stable stage of its life a star will change.

Describe and explain the changes that could take place.

53. Radioactive sources emit alpha, beta and gamma radiation.

(a) The diagram shows a radioactive source. In front of the source is a screen.

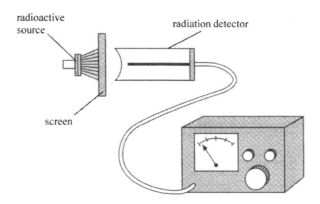

In each of the following cases state the type of radiation which is stopped by the screen.

Each type of radiation is to be used once only.

(i) What type of radiation is stopped when the screen is made of thick paper?

(ii) What other type of radiation is stopped when the screen is made of thick aluminium?

(iii) What other type of radiation is mainly stopped when the screen is made of thick lead?

(b) Very penetrating radiation is produced in nuclear reactors. Nuclear reactors are shielded with lead or concrete. The lead/concrete shielding does not stop all the radiation getting out.
Explain why shielding is important, even if it is only partially effective.

54. Radon has an atomic number of 86 and a mass number of 220. It emits an α-particle to become Polonium, which emits another α-particle to become a radioactive isotope of Lead.

The radioactive isotope of lead then emits a ß-particle to become Bismuth. What is (a) the atomic number and (b) the mass number of Bismuth?

55. A ratemeter records a background count rate of 2 counts per second. When a radioactive source is held near the count rate is 162 counts per second. If the half-life of the source is 5 min, what will the recorded count rate be 20 min later?

56. The diagrams below represent three atoms, A, B and C.

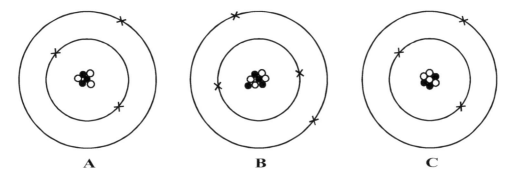

(a) Two of the atoms are from the same element.

(i) Which of A, B and C is an atom of a different element? ....

(ii) Give one reason for your answer.

(b)   Two of these atoms are isotopes of the same element.
(i)   Which two are isotopes of the same element? .... and ....

(ii)   Explain your answer.

57.(a) The graph shows how a sample of barium-143, a radioactive *isotope* with a short *half-life,* decays with time.

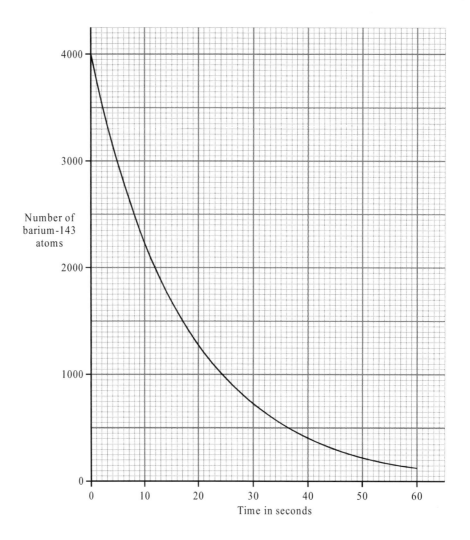

Number of barium-143 atoms

Time in seconds

(i)   What is meant by the term *isotope?*

(ii)   What is meant by the term *half-life?*

(iii)   Use the graph to find the half-life of barium-143.

Half-life = ... seconds

(b) Humans take in the radioactive isotope carbon-14 from their food. After their death, the proportion of carbon-14 in their bones can be used to tell how long it is since they died. Carbon-14 has a half-life of 5700 years.

(i) A bone in a living human contains 80 units of carbon-14. An identical bone taken from a skeleton found in an ancient burial ground contains 5 units of carbon-14. Calculate the age of the skeleton. Show clearly how you work out your answer.

(ii) Why is carbon-14 unsuitable for dating a skeleton believed to be about 150 years old?

58. The radioactive isotope, carbon-14, decays by beta particle emission.

(a) What is a beta particle?

(b) Plants absorb carbon-14 from the atmosphere. The graph shows the decay curve for 1 g of carbon-14 taken from a flax plant.

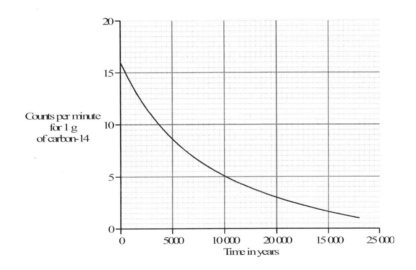

Use the graph to find the half-life of carbon-14. You should show clearly on your graph how you obtain your answer.

Half-life = ... years.

(c) Linen is a cloth made from the flax plant. A recent exhibition included part of a linen shirt, believed to have belonged to St. Thomas à Becket, who died in 1162. Extracting carbon-14 from the cloth would allow the age of the shirt to be verified.

If 1 g of carbon-14 extracted from the cloth were to give 870 counts in 1 hour, would it be possible for the shirt to have once belonged to St. Thomas à Becket? You must show clearly the steps used and reason for your decision.

59. (a) The table gives information about five radioactive isotopes.

Isotope	Type of radiation emitted	Half-life
Californium-241	alpha	4 minutes
Cobalt-60	gamma	5 years
Hydrogen-3	beta	12 years
Strontium-90	beta	28 years
Technetium-99	gamma	6 hours

(i)   What is an alpha particle?

(ii)   What is meant by the term half-life?

(iii) Which one of the isotopes could be used as a tracer in medicine? Explain the reason for your choice.

(b) The increased use of radioactive isotopes is leading to an increase in the amount of radioactive waste. One method for storing the waste is to seal it in containers which are then placed deep underground.

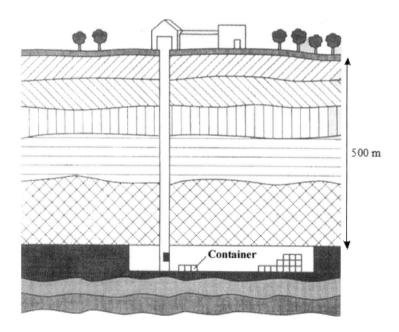

Some people may be worried about having such a storage site close to the area in which they live. Explain why.

60.(a)   The table shows the half-life of some *radioactive* isotopes.

Radioactive isotope	Half-life
magnesium-27	10 minutes
sodium-24	15 hours
sulphur-35	87 days
cobalt-60	5 years

(i) What is meant by the term *radioactive?*

(ii) Which one of the isotopes in the table could form part of a compound to be used as a tracer in medicine? Explain the reason for your choice.

(iii) Draw a graph to show how the number of radioactive atoms present in the isotope cobalt-60 will change with time.

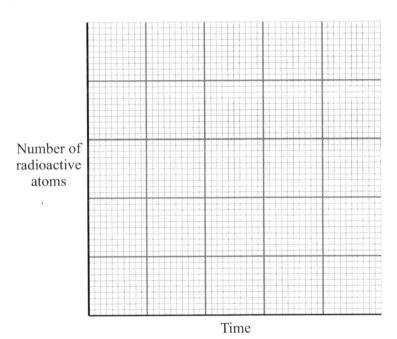

Number of radioactive atoms

Time

(b) Nuclear power stations provide about 17% of the world's electricity. They add less than 1% to the total background levels of radiation. Some people are opposed to the use of nuclear fuels for the generation of electricity. Explain why.

(c)Name and describe the process by which the Sun produces vast amounts of energy.

61. (a) The diagram shows a hazard sign.

What type of hazard does this sign warn you about?

(b) The names of three types of radiation are given in the box.

| alpha   beta   gamma |

Complete each sentence by choosing the correct type of radiation from those given in the box. Each type of radiation should be used once or not at all.

(i) The type of radiation that travels at the speed of light is ....

(ii) The type of radiation that is stopped by thick paper is ....

(c) The pie-chart shows the main sources of background radiation.

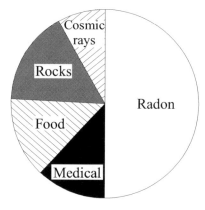

(i) Which source in the pie-chart adds the smallest amount of radiation to background levels?

(ii) Name two natural sources of background radiation in the pie-chart.

(d) The diagrams show how a radiation detector and counter can be used to measure radiation levels. In each case the numbers show the count one minute after the counter is switched on.

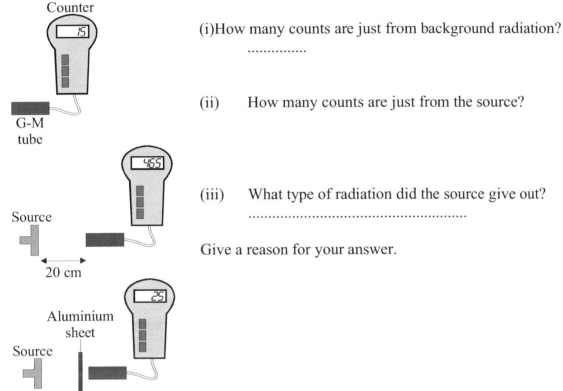

(i) How many counts are just from background radiation?

....

(ii) How many counts are just from the source?

(iii) What type of radiation did the source give out?

....

Give a reason for your answer.

62. (a) A radiation detector and counter were used to detect and measure the radiation emitted from a weak source. The graph shows how the number of counts recorded in one minute changed with time.

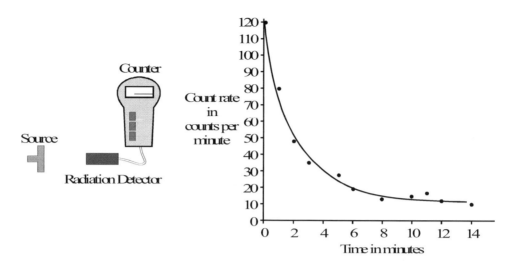

(i) Even though the readings from the counter were accurately recorded, not all the points fit the smooth curve. What does this tell us about the process of radioactive decay?

(ii) After ten minutes the number of counts recorded each minute is almost constant. Explain why.

(b) The radioactive isotope sodium-24 injected into the bloodstream can be used to trace blood flow to the heart. Sodium-24 emits both *beta particles* and *gamma rays*.

(i) What is a *beta particle*?

(ii) What is a *gamma ray*?

(iii) The count rate from a solution containing sodium-24 decreases from 584 counts per minute to 73 counts per minute in 45 hours. Calculate the half-life of sodium-2.2. Show clearly how you work out your answer.

63. A sample of radioactive material with a half life of 24 days has an initial activity recorded is 100 Bq. What is the activity after:
(a) 24 days
(b) 72 days

64. A sample of wood from an archaeological site is carbon dated. The activity is found to be 237 counts/gm/hour. If the initial activity of living wood is 950 counts/gm/hour how old is the wood sample. The half life of carbon 14 is 5570 years.

Revision Questions Answers

18 What is the current used by a 60 W lamp connected to a 240 V supply?

$$I = \frac{P}{V} = \frac{60}{240} = 0.25 \, A$$

19 Should a voltmeter have a high or low resistance? Explain your answer.

The voltmeter should have high resistance almost infinity. The voltmeter is connected in parallel.

$$\frac{1}{R_T} = \frac{1}{R_1} + \frac{1}{R_2}$$

If the resistance of voltmeter is ∞

$$\frac{1}{R_T} = \frac{1}{R_1} + \frac{1}{\infty}$$

$$\frac{1}{R_T} = \frac{1}{R_1}$$

$R_T = R$

Therefore, if the resistance of voltmeter is infinity, then the total resistance and current will not be affected.

20 Should an ammeter have a high or low resistance? Explain your answer.

The resistance of the ammeter should be very small almost zero. The ammeter is connected to the circuit in series. If resistance of the ammeter is zero, the total resistance of the circuit will not be affected.

21 Calculate the combined resistance of 2 Ω, 4 Ω and 6 Ω connected (a) in series; (b) in parallel.

$$R_T = R_1 + R_2 + R_3 = 2 + 4 + 6 = 12 \, \Omega$$

$$\frac{1}{R_T} = \frac{1}{R_1} + \frac{1}{R_2} + \frac{1}{R_3}$$

$$\frac{1}{R_T} = \frac{1}{2} + \frac{1}{4} + \frac{1}{6}$$

$$\frac{1}{R_T} = \frac{4 \times 6 + 2 \times 6 + 2 \times 4}{2 \times 4 \times 6} = \frac{24 + 12 + 8}{48} = \frac{44}{48}$$

$R_T = 1.09 \ \Omega$

22 What is the meaning of electromotive force (e.m.f.)?

Emf is equal to the energy converted to electrical energy by the cell per unit charge passing through it.

23 In the circuit below, what happens when the switch is closed, which lamps light? Calculate the total resistance of the circuit if resistance of each bulb is 200 Ω.

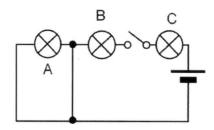

When the switch is closed, the bulb B and bulb C are in series.

$R_T = 200 + 200 = 400 \ \Omega$

Bulb A is short circuit.

24 In the circuit in below which lamps light when:
(a) S_1 is closed;
(b) S_1 and S_2 are closed?

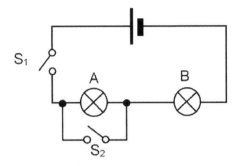

S_1 is closed, A and B are connected to the power supply. A and B are on.

A is short circuit, A is off. B is on.

25. What will the in each ammeter in circuits below?
All cells and lamps are identical.

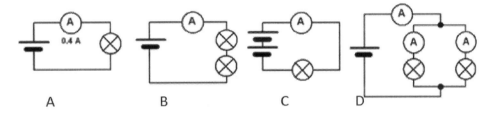

In circuit B, I = 0.2 A. In circuit C, I = 0.8 A. In circuit D, the total current = 0.8 A and in each branch 0.4 A.

26 How many joules of energy are given to 2 C by a 6 V battery?

$$E = QV = 2 \times 6 = 12\,J$$

27 How many joules of energy are used when a current of 100 A flows from a 8 V car battery for 10 s?

$$E = IVt = 100 \times 8 \times 10 = 8000\,J$$

28 Which uses more energy per second, a 100 W bulb running at 0.25 A or a 5 W bulb running at 0.25 A?

100 W Bulb uses 100 J each second. 5W bulb uses 5J each second.

29. Calculate how much electrical energy is supplied by a 12V battery when:
(a) a charge of 2000C passes through it
(b) a current of 5.5A flows from it for 75s

$$E = QV = 2000 \times 12 = 24000\,J$$

$$E = IVt = 5.5 \times 12 \times 75 = 4950\,J$$

30. How much energy is drawn from a 12V car battery if it is used to supply 120A for 10s to the starter motor.

$$E = IVt = 120 \times 12 \times 10 = 14400\,J$$

31. You have five 1.5V cells. Explain how you would connect them to give:
(a) the highest output potential

Connect them in series.

(b) a given current for the longest possible time

Connect them in parallel

(c) an output potential of 4.5V

Connect two batteries in a series and another two batteries in series. Then connect the series groups to each other in parallel, then finally connect the parallel group to another cell in series.

32. 20 identical light bulbs are connected in series across a 240V d.c supply.
(a) what is the p.d across each bulb
(b) what is the potential at the join of the second and third bulbs from the negative terminal?

Voltage across each = 240/20 = 12 V
Assuming bulb1 is connected to 240V potential. The potential between second and third is 216V.

33. Calculate the current through the following resistors:

(a) 4700 Ω connected to 12V
(b) 10kΩ connected to 24V
(c) 2.5MΩ connected to 3V

$$I = \frac{V}{R} = \frac{12}{4700} = 0.0025\ A$$
$$I = \frac{V}{R} = \frac{24}{10000} = 0.0024$$
$$I = \frac{V}{R} = \frac{3}{2.5 \times 10^6} = 1.2 \times 10^{-6}\ A$$

34. What is the resistance of the following?
(a) a torch bulb that draws 0.25 A from a 12V supply
(b) an immersion heater that draws 10 A from a 240V supply

a)

$$R = \frac{12}{0.25} = 48\ \Omega$$

b)

$$R = \frac{240}{10} = 24\ \Omega$$

*35 Two heating coils dissipate heat at the rate of 50 W and 100 W respectively when they are connected in series with a 12 V supply.

(a) What is the resistance of each coil?

(b) What would the total rate of heat dissipation become if they were then connected in series, their resistances remaining constant?

Using $P = \frac{V^2}{R}$, The resistance of 50 W resistance,

$$R = \frac{V^2}{P} = \frac{144}{50} = 28.8\ \Omega$$

The resistance of 100 W heater,

111

$$R = \frac{V^2}{P} = \frac{144}{100} = 14.4 \ \Omega$$

Connecting the two heaters in series, they will share the voltage. To find the heat generated by each we need to find the current or voltage across each.

$$R_t = R_1 + R_2 = 28.8 + 14.4 = 43.2 \ \Omega$$

$$I = \frac{12}{43.2} = 0.27 \ A$$

Power of 50W heater in series, $P = I^2 R = 0.27^2 \times 28.8 = 2.22 \ W$

Power of 100W heater in series, $P = I^2 R = 0.27^2 \times 14.4 = 1.11 \ W$

*36 A 12 V, 10W, bulb is connected in series with a 240 V, 60 W, bulb to the 240 V mains. Explain what will happen to both bulbs when the supply is switched on.

For this question, we need to find the resistance of each bulb,

$$R_1 = \frac{12^2}{10} = 14.4 \ \Omega$$

$$R_2 = \frac{240^2}{60} = 960 \ \Omega$$

$R_T = 960 + 14.4 = 974.4 \ \Omega$

The current through the circuit when both bulbs are connected in series = 240/974.4 = 0.24 A

For 12V, 10W bulb, the current for full brightness, $I = \frac{P}{V} = \frac{10}{12} = 0.83A$.

For 240 V, 60 W bulb, the current for full brightness, $I = \frac{P}{V} = \frac{60}{240} = 0.25A$

We can see from the above calculations, that the current is almost the same for 60W and the 240V bulb to be in full brightness. The 12V bulb, however, will very dim as the current is about third of the needed value for full brightness.

37 Two parallel resistances of 8 and 6 Ω are connected to the terminals of a battery consisting of four dry cells, each having an e.m.f. of 1.5 V in series (a) calculate the current through each resistor (b) the total current.

$$I_6 = \frac{6}{6} = 1\,A$$

$$I_8 = \frac{6}{8} = 0.75\,A$$

Total current = 1 + 0.75 = 1.75A

38. (a) The graph below shows how the current in two resistors, A and B, changes as voltage changes.

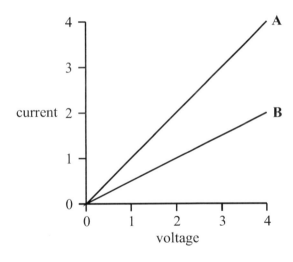

(i) How, if at all, does the resistance of resistor A change as voltage is increased?

Assuming the temperature of the conductor A is constant, then the resistance is constant.

(ii) How does the resistance of resistor B compare with that of resistor A?

The resistance of B is greater than the resistance of A

113

(b) The diagram shows a battery connected to two resistors.

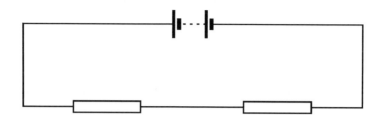

Complete the following sentence about the circuit.

The ....voltage .. from the battery is shared between the resistors whilst the same ...current . flows through each one.

(c) In this question all the cells are identical. Each cell has a voltage of 1.5 volts. The diagrams below show three ways of making a battery. In each case two cells are used.
Under each battery write the voltage you would expect the battery to have.

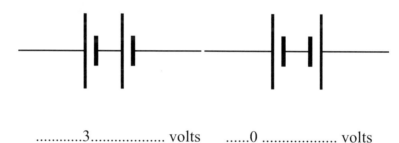

...........3.................... volts   ......0 .... volts

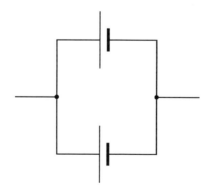

....1.5 .... volts

39. (a) A student is to design an electrical circuit which will indicate when the temperature inside an incubator is 40 °C.

114

(i) Name a suitable temperature sensor for the student to use.

Thermistor

(ii) Draw the circuit symbol for the temperature sensor you named above.

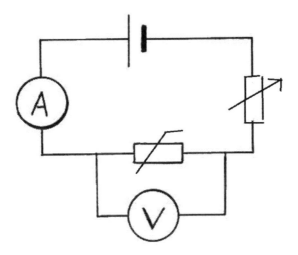

(b) Before designing the circuit the student measured the resistance of the sensor at different temperatures. The results are shown in the table.

Temperature in °C	Resistance of sensor in ohms
0	3000
10	2000
20	1400
30	1000
40	700
50	500

(i)   Draw a graph of these results.

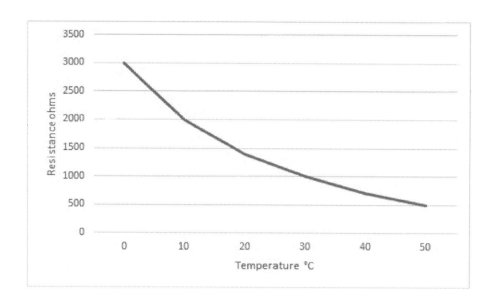

40. (a) The diagram shows the voltage-current graphs for three different electrical components.

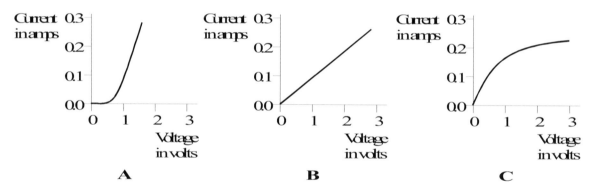

Which one of the components A, B or C could be a 3 volt filament lamp? Explain the reason for your choice.

C, the current through lamp increases, the temperature increases which result in increase in resistance. On graph the increase in resistance is showed by decrease in gradient of the curve.

(b) Using the correct symbols draw a circuit diagram to show how a battery, ammeter and voltmeter can be used to find the resistance of the wire shown.

116

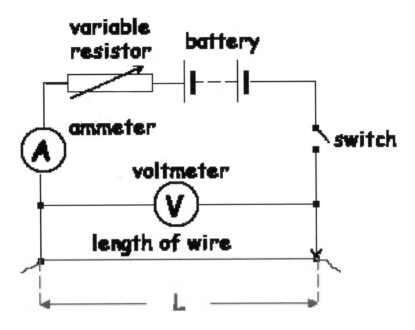

(c) When correctly connected to a 9 volt battery the wire has a current of 0.30 amperes flowing through it.

(i) Give the equation that links current, resistance and voltage.

....$Voltage = Current \times Resistance$......

(ii) Calculate the resistance of the wire. Show clearly how you work out your answer and give the unit.

.$Resistance = \frac{Voltage}{Current} = \frac{9}{0.3} = 30\ \Omega$

(iii) When the wire is heated, the current goes down to 0.26 amperes. State how the resistance of the wire has changed.

The resistance will increase.

.$Resistance = \frac{Voltage}{Current} = \frac{9}{0.26} = 34.6\ \Omega$

41.   The information plate on a hair drier is shown.

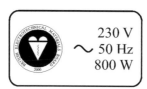

(a) What is the power rating of the hair drier?

800 W

(b) (i) Write down the equation which links current, power and voltage.

$$P = V \times I$$

(ii) Calculate the current in amperes, when the hair drier is being used. Show clearly how you work out your answer.

$$I = \frac{P}{V} = \frac{800}{230} = 3.47 \, A$$

(iii) Which one of the following fuses, 3A, 5A or 13A, should you use with this hair drier?

5A fuse

(c) The hair drier transfers electrical energy to heat energy and kinetic energy.

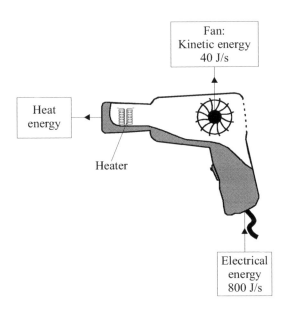

Use the following equation to calculate the efficiency of the hair drier in transferring electrical energy into heat energy.

$$efficiency = \frac{useful\,energy\,output}{total\,energy\,input}$$

$$efficiency = \frac{760}{800} = 95\%$$

42. The drawing shows someone ironing a shirt. The top of the ironing board is covered in a shiny silver-coloured material.

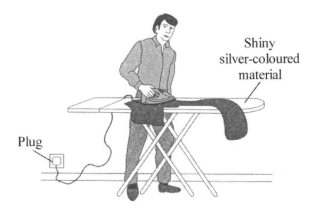

(a) Explain why the shiny silver-coloured material helps to make ironing easier.

Silver is a good reflector of heat radiation.

(b) The iron must be earthed to make it safe. Which part of the iron is connected to the earth pin of the plug?

Metal soleplate — Plastic part

The metal soleplate

(c) Name a material that could be used to make the outside case of the plug.

Give a reason for your choice.

Plastic or rubber. Good electrical insulator

43. (a) A steel nail may be magnetised by an electric current. Describe, with the aid of a diagram, how you would do this.

Wind a coil wire around a nail as in the diagram below. Connect the power supply to the dc current. Some of the magnetism produced by the wire will accumulate on the nail. If the current is left on for long enough, strong magnetism is generated.

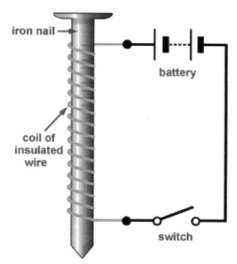

iron nail →

battery

coil of insulated wire

switch

(b) The diagram below shows a transformer.

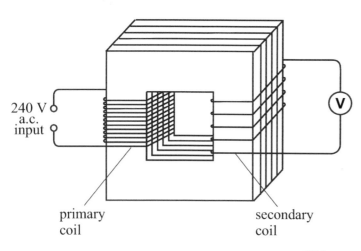

240 V a.c. input

V

primary coil

secondary coil

(i) Name the material used to make the core of the transformer.

Iron Core

(ii) The primary coil has 48 000 turns and the secondary coil 4000 turns.
If the input voltage is 240 V a.c., calculate the output voltage.

$$\frac{N_p}{N_s} = \frac{V_p}{V_s}$$

$$\frac{48000}{4000} = \frac{240}{V_s}$$

$$V_s = \frac{240 \times 4000}{48000} = 20\ V$$

(iii) Explain how the use of such a transformer could be adapted to transform a low voltage into a higher voltage.

Revise input to output.

44. The outline diagram below shows part of the National Grid. At **X** the transformer increases the voltage to a very high value. At **Y** the voltage is reduced to 240 V for use by consumers.

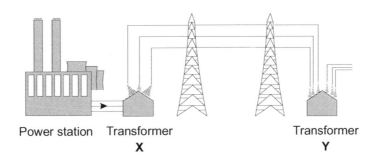

Power station   Transformer
X

Transformer
Y

(i) The frequency of the mains supply to houses is 50 Hz. Explain what this means.
.

The current reverse direction 50 times a second.....

(ii) At **X** a transformer increases the voltage. What happens to the current as the voltage is increased?

The current decreases and voltage increases .

(iii) Why is electrical energy transmitted at very high voltages?

With high voltage, the current is very small. Less energy is wasted as heat as the current is small current

(iv) The transformer at **Y** reduces the voltage before it is supplied to houses. Why is this done?

For safety reason, we can't use high voltage.

45. The diagram below shows an electric generator.

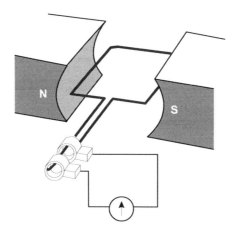

(a) What must be done to the generator to enable it to produce electricity?

The coil must be rotated

(b) Why is a voltage induced in the coil?

The coil is cutting magnetic field lines which results in an electrical potential difference is induced across the ends of the wire

(c) Give **four** ways in which the size of the induced voltage could be increased if another generator was built.

1. *speed of rotation;*
2. *strength of field*
3. *soft iron core;*
4. *number of coil turns;*
5. *coil area*

46. (a) In the diagram below a magnet, attached to a spring, is free to vibrate in a coil of wire.

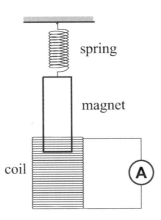

When the magnet is pushed down and released its vibrations rapidly die away.

The magnet is now replaced by an iron bar, the same size and mass as the magnet. When this is pushed down the same distance and released its vibrations take considerably longer to die away.

Explain why the vibrations of the magnet did not last as long as those of the iron bar.

As a magnet vibrates, a changing magnetic field will be induced. This will interact with the coil, producing an induced current and that will induce electromagnetism. The induced electromagnetism will damp the vibration of the magnet.

(b)   The diagram below shows a dynamo suitable for use on a cycle.

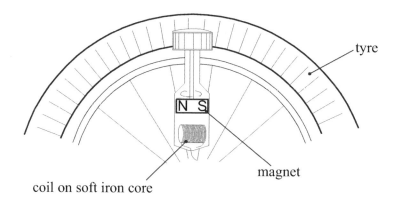

tyre

N S

magnet

coil on soft iron core

(i) Explain why a voltage is generated when the dynamo is turned by the tyre.

As the magnet rotates gives changing field in coil. Therefore, an induces voltage and current

(ii) Explain why the brightness of the lamp increases as the cyclist goes faster.

The magnetic field changes more quickly so induced higher voltage to lamp.

(iii) Describe **three** changes you would make to the design of the dynamo if you wanted it to generate a bigger voltage.

    1. Stronger magnet

    2. More turns on coil

    3. magnet spin faster by using smaller knurled top

47. The diagram shows apparatus used to demonstrate the motor effect. **X** is a short length of bare copper wire resting on two other wires.

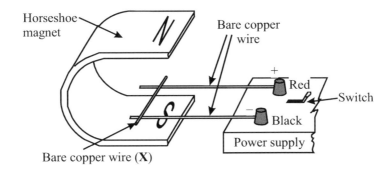

(a)(i)   Describe what happens to wire **X** when the current is switched on.

Using the left-hand rule, we can see that, the wire moves towards the right.

(ii) What difference do you notice if the following changes are made?

A The magnetic field is reversed.

The wire moves in opposite direction, towards the left.

B The current is increased.

The increase in current will results in increase in force on the wire, the wire will move faster.

(b) The diagram shows a coil placed between the poles of a magnet. The arrows on the sides of
the coil itself show the direction of the conventional current.

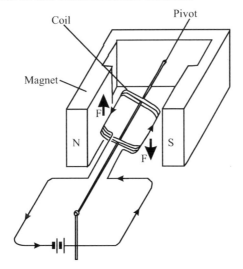

The arrows labelled **F** show the direction of the forces acting on the sides of the coil. Describe the motion of the coil until it comes to rest.

The coil turns clockwise while the coil cutting the field lines. The coil will come to rest when facing field at 90°.

(c) Most electric motors use electromagnets instead of permanent magnets. State three of the features of an electromagnet which control the strength of the magnetic field obtained.

    1. number of turns
    2. current
    3. Iron core

48. The diagram below shows a coil of wire connected to a meter which can measure small currents.

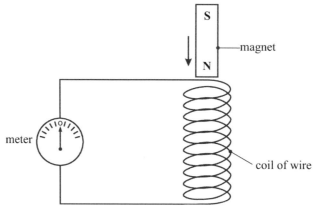

(a) What, if anything, happens to the needle of the meter as the magnet is moved into the coil?

The ammeter needle will move and will register a reading

(b) The magnet is now left stationary inside the coil as shown in the diagram below.

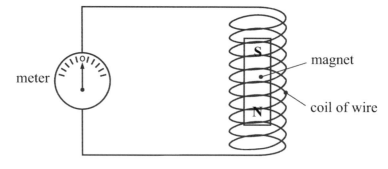

What, if anything, happens to the needle of the meter?

The ammeter needle will show zero .

(c) What, if anything, happens to the needle of the meter as the magnet is lifted out of the coil?

The ammeter needle will move will deflect. The deflection of the needle will be opposite to that when the magnet was pushed into the coil

49. The diagram below shows a door lock which can be opened from a flat inside a building.

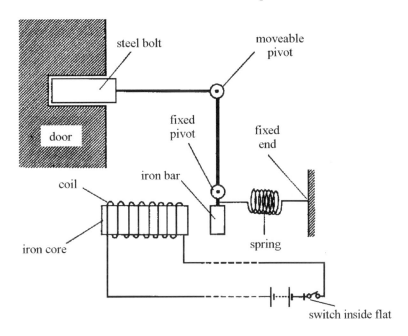

(a) Explain how the door is unlocked when the switch is closed.

The circuit will turn on, current flows through the coil which make it electromagnet. The electromagnet attracts iron bar causing bolt to be pulled out.
(b) State **two** changes which would increase the strength of the electromagnet.

    1. more turns
    2. bigger current or e.m.f
    3. softer iron core

(c)   Why is the spring needed in the lock?

To return iron bar and lock door.

(d) The connections to the coil were accidentally reversed. Would the lock still work?

The iron bar would still be attracted as coil still be magnetised, so still works

50. A patient suffering from cancer of the thyroid gland is given a dose of radioactive iodine 131, with a half-life of 8 days, to combat the disease. He is temporarily radioactive, and his nurses must be changed regularly to protect them. If his radioactivity is initially 4 times the acceptable level, how long is it before the special nursing rota can be dropped?

Two half lives is enough to get the level of radiation to normal. Two half lives equals 16 days.

51. Stars are formed from massive clouds of dust and gases in space.

(a) What force pulls the clouds of dust and gas together to form stars?

Gravitational attraction

(b) Once formed a star can have a stable life for billions of years. Describe the two main forces at work in the star during this period of stability.

Gravitational force in, high internal temperature generates force, out.

(c) What happens to this star once this stable period is over?

Star expands; to form red giant. After the red giant, the core will collapse; to form white dwarf or neutron star or black hole.

(d) Suggest what might then happen to a planet close to this star.

Engulfed by red giant.

52. (a) The Sun is at the stable stage of its life.

Explain, in terms of the forces acting on the Sun, what this means.

The Sun is subject to two balancing forces, the forces are: gravity making it contract and a force due to heat energy or radiation pressure making it expand.

(b) At the end of the stable stage of its life a star will change.

Describe and explain the changes that could take place.

When the hydrogen fuel runs out in the core of the star, the star will collapse. The outer core will heat up enough for a fusion reaction to happen in the outer core. It will result in the outer shells expanding and becoming a red giant. When all hydrogen has run out, the star will contract under gravity to become a white dwarf. For very large stars, the star may explode and become a supernova, throwing dust and gas into space, leaving a dense neutron star or black hole.

53. Radioactive sources emit alpha, beta and gamma radiation.

(a) The diagram shows a radioactive source. In front of the source is a screen.

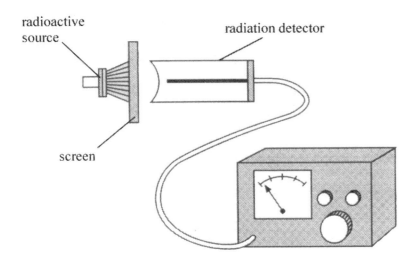

In each of the following cases state the type of radiation which is stopped by the screen.

Each type of radiation is to be used once only.

(i) What type of radiation is stopped when the screen is made of thick paper?

Alpha

(ii) What other type of radiation is stopped when the screen is made of thick aluminium?

Beta

(iii) What other type of radiation is mainly stopped when the screen is made of thick lead?

Gamma

(b) Very penetrating radiation is produced in nuclear reactors. Nuclear reactors are shielded with lead or concrete. The lead/concrete shielding does not stop all the radiation getting out. Explain why shielding is important, even if it is only partially effective.

Having a lead shield will reduce the radiation to allow workers to maintain the reactor without being exposed to large radiation doses. Without the shield, the amount of radiation will reach a lethal dose in minutes.

54. Radon has an atomic number of 86 and a mass number of 220. It emits an α-particle to become Polonium, which emits another α-particle to become a radioactive isotope of Lead.
The radioactive isotope of lead then emits a ß-particle to become Bismuth. What is (a) the atomic number and (b) the mass number of Bismuth?

Atomic number = 83

Mass number = 212

55. A ratemeter records a background count rate of 2 counts per second. When a radioactive source is held near the count rate is 162 counts per second. If the half-life of the source is 5 min, what will the recorded count rate be 20 min later?

Count rate = 162-2 = 160

20 minutes = 4 half lives

Count rate after 20 minutes = 160 /16 = 10 Bq

56. The diagrams below represent three atoms, A, B and C.

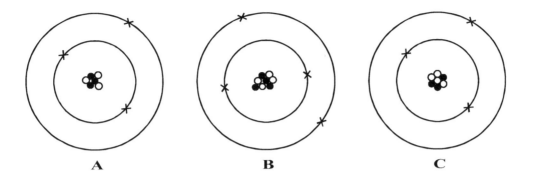

A   **B**   **C**

(a) Two of the atoms are from the same element.

(i) Which of A, B and C is an atom of a different element? ....B.........

(ii) Give one reason for your answer.

B has different number of protons.

(b)   Two of these atoms are isotopes of the same element.
(i)   Which two are isotopes of the same element? ....A........... and .....C..........

(ii)   Explain your answer.
They have the same number of protons and different number of neutrons

57.(a)   The graph shows how a sample of barium-143, a radioactive *isotope* with a short *half-life,* decays with time.

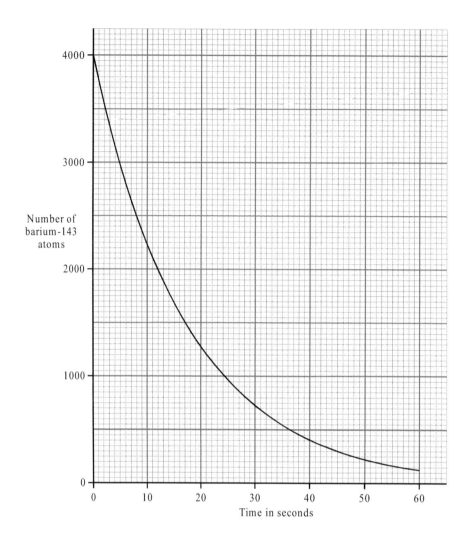

Time in seconds

(i)   What is meant by the term *isotope?*

Atoms which have the same number of proton and different numbers neutrons.

(ii)   What is meant by the term *half-life*?

The time taken for half of radioactive nuclei to decay.

(iii)   Use the graph to find the half-life of barium-143.

Half-life = ...12.............. seconds

(b) Humans take in the radioactive isotope carbon-14 from their food. After their death, the proportion of carbon-14 in their bones can be used to tell how long it is since they died. Carbon-14 has a half-life of 5700 years.

(i) A bone in a living human contains 80 units of carbon-14. An identical bone taken from a skeleton found in an ancient burial ground contains 5 units of carbon-14. Calculate the age of the skeleton. Show clearly how you work out your answer.

$$A = \frac{A_0}{2^n}$$

$$5 = \frac{80}{2^n}$$

$$2^n = 16$$

$n = 4$

Age of skeleton $= 4 \times 5700 = 22800$ years

(ii) Why is carbon-14 unsuitable for dating a skeleton believed to be about 150 years old?

Very little decay has had happened in 150 years.

150 is 1/38 of the half life

58. The radioactive isotope, carbon-14, decays by beta particle emission.
(a) What is a beta particle?

Electron

(b) Plants absorb carbon-14 from the atmosphere. The graph shows the decay curve for 1 g of carbon-14 taken from a flax plant.

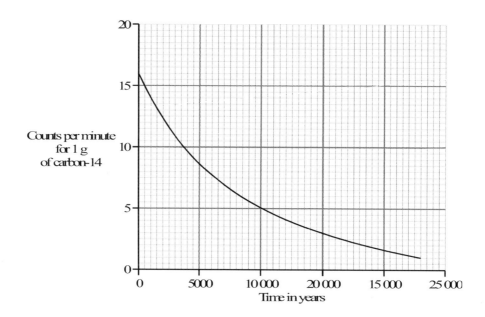

Use the graph to find the half-life of carbon-14. You should show clearly on your graph how you obtain your answer.

Half-life = ...6000................ years.

(c) Linen is a cloth made from the flax plant. A recent exhibition included part of a linen shirt, believed to have belonged to St. Thomas à Becket, who died in 1162. Extracting carbon-14 from the cloth would allow the age of the shirt to be verified.

If 1 g of carbon-14 extracted from the cloth were to give 870 counts in 1 hour, would it be possible for the shirt to have once belonged to St. Thomas à Becket? You must show clearly the steps used and reason for your decision.

Count rate per minute = 870/60 = 14.5 for each 1 g

The time difference between date today and date of death of Becket = 2019 – 1162 = 857 years

Using ratios

$$\frac{0.5}{x} = \frac{5700}{857}$$

x = 0.075

134

Activity per minute from 1g of the shirt = 14.5 - 0.075 × 14.5 = 13.4

Yes, it is possible

59. (a) The table gives information about five radioactive isotopes.

Isotope	Type of radiation emitted	Half-life
Californium-241	alpha	4 minutes
Cobalt-60	gamma	5 years
Hydrogen-3	beta	12 years
Strontium-90	beta	28 years
Technetium-99	gamma	6 hours

(i) What is an alpha particle?

The nucleus of helium, two protons and two neutrons.

(ii) What is meant by the term half-life?

The time taken for the radioactive nuclei to decrease to half.

(iii) Which one of the isotopes could be used as a tracer in medicine? Explain the reason for your choice.

Technetium-99

We need a gamma emitter and suitable short half-life or activity quickly reduced to a safe level or it doesn't stay in the body long.

(b) The increased use of radioactive isotopes is leading to an increase in the amount of radioactive waste. One method for storing the waste is to seal it in containers which are then placed deep underground.

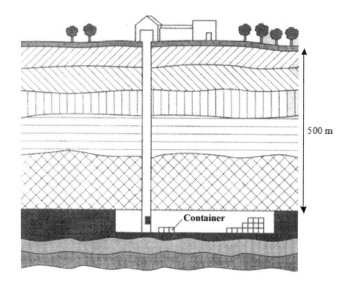

Some people may be worried about having such a storage site close to the area in which they live. Explain why.

Possible leakage or contamination of land or water increases the risk of radiation which are linked to illness or cancer.

60.(a) The table shows the half-life of some *radioactive* isotopes.

Radioactive isotope	Half-life
magnesium-27	10 minutes
sodium-24	15 hours
sulphur-35	87 days
cobalt-60	5 years

(i) What is meant by the term *radioactive?*

An unstable nucleus

(ii) Which one of the isotopes in the table could form part of a compound to be used as a tracer in medicine? Explain the reason for your choice.

Sodium – 24, the half life is short enough that levels of radiation in the body will become very small quickly

(iii) Draw a graph to show how the number of radioactive atoms present in the isotope cobalt-60 will change with time.

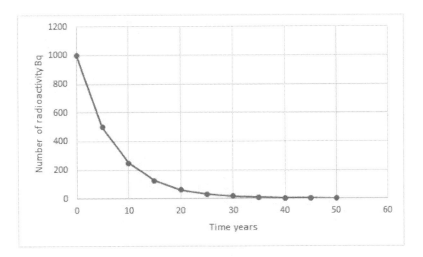

(b) Nuclear power stations provide about 17% of the world's electricity. They add less than 1% to the total background levels of radiation. Some people are opposed to the use of nuclear fuels for the generation of electricity. Explain why.

The waste remains radioactive for a long time. The waste must be disposed of and may leak which results in contamination of the local environment. People living close to a power station may have a greater risk of developing cancer or leukaemia

(c)Name and describe the process by which the Sun produces vast amounts of energy.

Nuclear fusion. Hydrogen is converted to helium, generating a large amount of energy.

61. (a) The diagram shows a hazard sign.

What type of hazard does this sign warn you about?

Radioactivity.

(b) The names of three types of radiation are given in the box.

alpha   beta   gamma

Complete each sentence by choosing the correct type of radiation from those given in the box. Each type of radiation should be used once or not at all.

(i) The type of radiation that travels at the speed of light is ...Gamma

(ii)   The type of radiation that is stopped by thick paper is .Beta .

(c)   The pie-chart shows the main sources of background radiation.

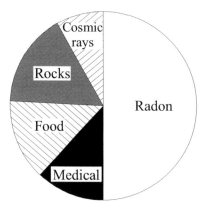

(i) Which source in the pie-chart adds the smallest amount of radiation to background levels?

Cosmic rays

(ii) Name two natural sources of background radiation in the pie-chart.

Rocks, Food,

(d) The diagrams show how a radiation detector and counter can be used to measure radiation levels. In each case the numbers show the count one minute after the counter is switched on.

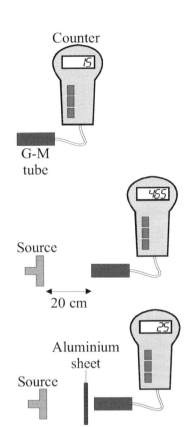

(i)   How many counts are just from background radiation?

.......15.....

(ii)   How many counts are just from the source?

.465-15 = 450 Bq..

(iii)   What type of radiation did the source give out?

..Betas...

Give a reason for your answer.

Alpha could not reach GM tube. Gamma can penetrate the GM tube without been detected.

62. (a) A radiation detector and counter were used to detect and measure the radiation emitted from a weak source. The graph shows how the number of counts recorded in one minute changed with time.

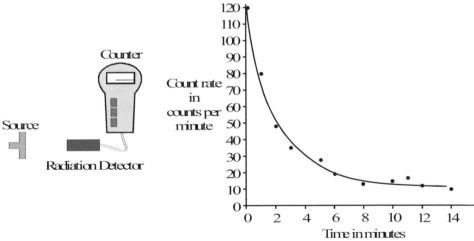

(i) Even though the readings from the counter were accurately recorded, not all the points fit the smooth curve. What does this tell us about the process of radioactive decay?

Radioactivity is random process

(ii) After ten minutes the number of counts recorded each minute is almost constant. Explain why.

Record background radiation.

(b) The radioactive isotope sodium-24 injected into the bloodstream can be used to trace blood flow to the heart. Sodium-24 emits both *beta particles* and *gamma rays*.

(i) What is a *beta particle?*

Electron

(ii) What is a *gamma ray?*

Electromagnetic wave with high frequency

(iii) The count rate from a solution containing sodium-24 decreases from 584 counts per minute to 73 counts per minute in 45 hours. Calculate the half-life of sodium-2.2. Show clearly how you work out your answer.

$$A = \frac{A_0}{2^n}$$

$$73 = \frac{584}{2^n}$$

n = 3

$$T_{\frac{1}{2}} = 15 \ hours$$

63. A sample of radioactive material with a half life of 24 days has an initial activity recorded is 100 Bq. What is the activity after:
(a) 24 days
(b) 72 days

   a) 50 Bq
   b) 12 Bq

64. A sample of wood from an archaeological site is carbon dated. The activity is found to be 237 counts/gm/hour. If the initial activity of living wood is 950 counts/gm/hour how old is the wood sample. The half life of carbon 14 is 5570 years.

$$A = \frac{A_0}{2^n}$$

$$237 = \frac{950}{2^n}$$

$2^n = 4$

$n = 2$

Time $= 2 \times 5570 = 11140$ years

Manufactured by Amazon.ca
Bolton, ON

14514016R00081